DYNAMIC JEWISH LAW

PROGRESSIVE HALAKHAH

Essence and Application

STUDIES IN PROGRESSIVE HALAKHAH, VOLUME I

PROGRESSIVE HALAKHAH

Essence and Application

Edited by
Walter Jacob and Moshe Zemer

Freehof Institute of Progressive Halakhah
Tel Aviv and Pittsburgh
Rodef Shalom Press
1991

Published by the Rodef Shalom Press
4905 5th Avenue
Pittsburgh, PA 15213
U.S.A.

4 Rehov Levitan
69204 Tel Aviv
Israel

4905 5th Avenue
Pittsburgh, PA 15213
U.S.A.

Library of Congress Catalog Card Number 91-60867

Jacob, Walter 1930-

Zemer, Moshe 1932-

ISBN 0-929699-03-3

This Volume is dedicated to

the memory of

Solomon B. Freehof

for whom this Institute has been named

Table of Contents

Introduction

Progressive *halakhah** is based on a scientific and historic approach to the Jewish tradition which leads modern scholars to affirm the developmental character of Scripture and rabbinic literature. Revelation is a divine-human encounter rather than the transmission of infallible law by God to human beings. Progressive *halakhah*, therefore, is founded on a non-fundamentalist reinterpretation of revelation. Critical investigation of the classic sources demonstrates diversity, flexibility, and creativity in Jewish law. Earlier studies reveal principles and criteria for determining the *mitzvot* for our time. Such criteria of Liberal *halakhah* will, among other things, 1) give priority to ethical dimensions in applying *mitzvot* to life, 2) view *kedushah* (holiness) as a rationale for evaluating commandments, and 3) provide some role to the individual conscience in determining *halakhic* choice.

Progressive *halakhah* has developed greatly during the last five decades. This has occurred in the United States, Europe and Israel. The impetus in this direction came as the American Reform movement moved from its more radical earlier positions.

The need for a new approach to *halakhah* had not been felt by the large pre-war Central European Liberal community. As that community had not participated in a sharp break with the Tradition, it did not need to discover new ways of returning to it. This meant that no clearly identifiable Reform or Liberal Jewish approach to *halakhah* was developed by that creative community. There was a strong interest in historical studies like those of Geiger and Frankel which set a theoretical foundation for *halakhic* changes, however, in the succeeding generations no practical Liberal *halakhah* developed.

---

* The terms Progressive *halakhah*, Reform *halakhah*, and Liberal *halakhah* are used interchangeably throughout this book.

Matters were different in America. The nineteenth and early twentieth century had witnessed a rebellion against *halakhic* strictures. By the second decade of the twentieth century, however, a change had become visible in the debates of the Central Conference of American Rabbis. The position developed by the Columbus Platform (1937) and the newly revised Union Prayerbook (1940) demonstrated a new mood. A need for practically expressed standards of ethics and observance began to be felt. This was expressed through the work of Solomon B. Freehof's *Reform Jewish Practice*, vols. I (1944), and II (1952) as well as a similar effort by David Polish and Max Doppelt. In the subsequent decades the field of Reform Responsa was developed by Solomon B. Freehof, and *halakhic* discussions became more common in the *Journal of Reform Judaism*, volumes of responsa published by the Central Conference as well as other forums.

In the years following the Second World War, similar interests in *halakhah* began to be shown by the Reform, Progressive and Liberal Jewish communities of England and various other countries. In Israel the developing Progressive movement undertook its own effort in this direction. During the past two decades, numerous articlrs, written in the spirit of Liberal *halakhah*, were published in the national Hebrew press. For the most part these efforts were conducted by rabbis working alone or in the framework of their own movement with little relationship to Reform *halakhists* in other part of the world. In order to establish cooperation among Liberal *halakhic* scholars and lay-persons, the Freehof Institute of Progressive *Halakhah* was established in 1990. It is an affiliate of the World Union for Progressive Judaism.

The Freehof Institute of Progressive *Halakhah* is a creative research center devoted to studying and defining the progressive character of the *halakhah* in accordance with the principles and theology of Reform Judaism. It will work to establish the ideological basis of Progressive *halakhah*, and its application to daily life. The Institute hopes to foster serious studies, and to help

6

scholars in the Reform, Liberal, and Progressive rabbinate along with some Conservative and Orthodox colleagues as well as university professors serve on our Academic Council. The contributors to this volume are members of this Council.

This collection of essays is the product of the founding colloquium held in London during May 1990. This book is the first in a series which will explore different areas and seek to lead us closer to these goals. The subjects are diverse and the approaches taken by the authors are equally so. We wish to encourage a wide ranging discussion as well as the exploration of contemporary and historic themes.

The editors wish to thank the Rodef Shalom Congregation of Pittsburgh, PA for its continuing support which has made the publication of this volume possible. We also thank Regitze W. Hamburger for her editorial assistance as well as Tina Herman, Barbara W. Bailey, and Leon A. Morris for their work on the manuscript.

Moshe Zemer   Walter Jacob
Tel Aviv   Pittsburgh

Authority and Criteria in Liberal *Halakhah*

Moshe Zemer

I. The Authority of Liberal Halakhah

In order to establish criteria for *pesikah*, we must first clarify our view of the authority of the *halakhah*. This question of *halakhic* authority is perhaps the major source of contention between Progressive and Orthodox decisors. The Orthodox view may well be represented by the Chief Rabbinate of Israel in its 1984 brief to the Supreme Court of Israel in the case of the Israel Movement for Progressive Judaism against the Rabbinate for the right to officiate at marriages and to register them.

The Chief Rabbinic Council contended that Jewish Law derives its divine authority from the absolute dominion of the Mosaic Law given in Sinai. According to their brief, a *halakhic* Jew is one "who considers himself bound by the Torah (*kavul alyedei hatorah* - literally 'chained' by the Torah) that was given to Moses in Sinai, and sees himself chained by the words of the sages of the generations and the decisors of *halakhah* during the entirety of Jewish history..."[1] In this view, any non-Orthodox Jew who does not see himself so chained by the Torah is disqualified as a *halakhic* Jew.

In reply, I filed, on behalf of our movement, a *halakhic* brief with the Supreme Court which noted that the Chief Rabbinate's position is based on a literalist interpretation of Biblical texts and rabbinical sources. These gentlemen cling to the doctrine of the early Mishnaic period which propounds that Scripture "teaches that the Torah, its laws and details and interpretations were all given through Moses on Sinai."[2]

Since everything was revealed on the Mount, the Talmudic

conclusion seems inevitable that "no prophet is permitted to innovate in any matter from this time forth."[3] If this is true of the prophets, then *kal vahomer* it certainly applies to the rabbis, because "the pronouncement that a veteran student will make in the future before his teacher has already been given to Moses on Sinai."[4]

It is this fundamentalist position that leads most Orthodox thinkers to reject the historical and scientific view of the developmental character of Scripture and rabbinic literature held by Progressive Jewish scholars.

Among the innumerable sources which support the developmental approach, we might refer to the famous Talmudic *aggadah* of Moses visiting the Academy of Rabbi Akiba, where he fails to understand the second century Tanna's interpretations of Scripture. Only when a student asks Akiba for the source of his teaching and Akiba responds: *halakhah lemosheh misinai*, does Moses recognize in Akiba's *midrash halakhah* a continuation of his own teaching.[5]

Louis Jacobs interprets this passage as meaning that "the Torah that Akiba was teaching was so different from the Torah given to Moses-- because the social, economic, political and religious conditions were so different in Akiba's day that, at first, Moses could not recognize his Torah in the Torah taught by Akiba. But he was reassured when he realized that Akiba's Torah was implicit in his Torah, was, indeed an attempt to make his Torah relevant to the spiritual needs of Jews in the age of Akiba."[6]

By analyzing this and many other passages, liberal scholars have reached the conclusion "that long before the rise of modern criticism some of the Jewish teachers had a conception of revelation which leaves room for the idea of human cooperation with the divine."[6a] How indeed is the divine will revealed in *halakhah*?

10

Jacobs propounds that "revelation must be understood as a far more complicated and complex process of divine-human encounter and interaction and quite differently from the idea of direct divine communication of infallible laws and propositions, upon which the traditional theory of the *halakhah* depends."[7]

A progressive *halakhah* must therefore be founded on such a reinterpretation of revelation. Of course, this theological-*halakhic* position is unacceptable to the Orthodox rabbinate, because it has far reaching ramifications for the authority of the traditional *halakhah*. As Jacobs contends, for the non-Orthodox Jew, "the ultimate authority for determining which observances are binding upon the faithful Jew is the historical experience of the people of Israel, since, historically perceived, this is ultimately the sanction of the *halakhah* itself."[8]

We must therefore conclude that a serious Progressive Jew accepts or rejects the content of tradition, not out of convenience or caprice, but rather from a liberal theological *Weltanschauung* on revelation, history and *halakhah*.

If this be the source of Liberal Jewish authority, then what are the criteria and principles that enable the non-Orthodox Jew to choose *mitzvot* and *halakhot* that are valid and meaningful in the framework of Progressive *halakhah*?

II.   Principles and Criteria of Liberal Halakhah

Our theological position on the authority of the *halakhah* together with sensitivity to the ethical, to inner spirituality and to social justice are determining factors in the application of a particular *mitzvah* to a specific case. Some of the foremost thinkers of this century have presented us with criteria of the observance of *mitzvot* by the non-fundamentalist Jew which are essential to the

11

liberal process of rendering *halakhic* decisions. Most Orthodox decisors would probably reject these criteria, because the very process of choosing commandments runs contrary to the traditional view of the absolute authority of the divinely derived and sanctioned *halakhah*.

The following principles and criteria for determining the applicable *halakhic* stance for a Progressive Jew were gleaned from a number of Jewish thinkers of this century. Some of them are identified as Progressive scholars, others as Orthodox or Conservative. Their approach to *halakhah* rather than movement affiliation determines their inclusion in this paper. Here is a brief outline of precepts and criteria for *pesikah*, (rendering decisions) and selecting viable *mitzvot* to be observed within a liberal *halakhic* framework:

1. The *halakhah* is a developmental and changing phenomenon

In the brief that I submitted to the Israel Supreme Court to counter the Chief Rabbinate's view of the immutability of Jewish law, I contended that "The *halakhah* has continually developed and changed in confronting changing reality in every generation." The history of Jewish law from the Biblical period to this day is replete with changes such as substituting study and prayer for sacrifices, to upgrading the status of women (no *kidushin* or divorce without feminine consent) to allowing conversion for the sake of marriage.[9]

These are but a few of a myriad developments within the *halakhah*, which, according to Robert Gordis, result from outward influences and inner ethical insights. Gordis points out that these two factors have contributed to growth and change in the *halakhah*: "The first was the necessity to respond to new external conditions-- social, economic, political or cultural that posed a challenge or even a threat to accepted religious and ethical values. The second was the need to give recognition to new ethical insights and attitudes

12

and to embody them in the life of the people..."[10] This concept of change and development may serve as a guideline for the modern Jew in judging those *mitzvot* that developed with the changing times and are therefore relevant to our day. This criterion would put aside commandments such as *halitzah* which might have had some relevancy in the distant past, but have no spiritual meaning, even if reinterpreted, for the modern Jew.

2. The *halakhah* is pluralistic

A corollary of the developmental aspect of the *halakhah* is its pluralist character. Historical research proves that Jewish law was diverse in character and certainly far from monolithic. In the controversy between Beit Hillel and Beit Shammai on forbidden marriages, the two Houses did not refrain from marrying one another, even though such marriages might be forbidden according to the *halakhic* decision of either.[11] Yitzhak Gilat, professor of Talmud at Bar Ilan University, points out that in spite of the great differences between the Houses, they came to the recognition that "both are the words of the living God,"[12] and that everyone could act according to either view: "Whoever wishes to conduct himself according to Beit Shammai- may do so, and according to Beit Hillel- may do so."[13]

This freedom of *halakhic* ruling was accepted in practice during the time of the Second Temple; Professor Gilat claims: "Every sage was permitted to render decisions in his town and home according to his own tradition and in consonance with his judgement arising from deliberations in the rabbinic sources." We may therefore conclude that we have here a firmly based principle for *pesikah*: Since pluralism has been an intrinsic characteristic of Jewish religious life, one can legitimately choose the practices of any accepted Jewish religious tradition, including those of the non-Orthodoxy.

3. The ethical is the priority of *halakhah*

Eliezer Berkovits proclaims: "The rabbis in the Talmud were guided by the insight: God forbid that there should be anything in the application of the Torah to the actual life situation that is contrary to the principles of ethics." [14] If a ruling is *halakhic*, it must be ethical. If it is unethical, it cannot be *halakhic*.

Seymour Siegel applies this principle of priority to the practice of selecting, revising or abolishing particular laws. He proclaims: "The ethical values of our tradition should have the power to judge the particulars of Jewish law. If any law in our tradition does not fulfill our ethical values, then the law should be abolished or revised... Thus, if because of changing conditions, the specific laws no longer express the ethical values which Tradition teaches,... we have the responsibility to revise the laws, rather than allow them to fall into desuetude."[15] Siegel would apply this principle to matters involving *mamzerut*, the marriage of a *kohen* to a divorcee or convert, the refusal to give a get and similar cases.

We should likewise apply this ethical principle to issues of social justice in our respective countries. For example, there should be a liberal *halakhic* approach to the moral issues of the *Intifada* and demolishing the family homes of suspected terrorists.[16]

4. Holiness is the reason for the commandments

Julius Guttman deals with general rationale of the *mitzvah* (*taam hamitzvah*) rather than with the reason for each individual commandment. He states that *kedushah* (holiness) is the reason for the commandment character of Judaism. The Torah bears witness to the general purpose of the *mitzvah*: "That you may remember and do all my commandments and be holy to your God...The origin of the commandments is in the idea of *kedushah*."[17]

The *mitzvah* is not an end unto itself but a means by which one may be sanctified and drawn closer to God. The possibility of attaining *kedushah* is one of the criteria of the observance of a commandment. *Mitzvot* such as prayer, study of Torah, *gemilut hasadim* and others should lead to sanctification. The litmus test of holiness should determine the value of every religious act for the daily life of the Jew of our generation.

5. Internalizing the *mitzvah*

How does a particular *mitzvah* become part and parcel of one's inner being? Franz Rosenzweig suggested a progression from "Ich muss" to "Ich kann" - from "I am obliged" to observe because of an outer demand to "I am able" to fulfill the *mitzvah* because of an inner calling. What I am not yet able to accept may, in time, become acceptable, and therefore a commandment for me. The criterion of the observance of a commandment is whether I may internalize and observe this *mitzvah bekavanah,* with inner devotion and intent. This requires a constant effort of selecting and trying *mitzvot.* This is undoubtedly what Rosenzweig meant in his reported reply to the query, Do you put on *tefilin?* When he responded: "Noch nicht" - Not yet. In the words of Franz Rosenzweig: "...the voice of commandment causes the spark to leap from 'I must' to 'I can.' The Law is built on such commandments and only on them."[18]

6. The critical approach to the *halakhah*

John Rayner clearly expounded the following infrequently expressed principle of Liberal *halakhah*: "There are whole vast areas of *halakhah*...predicated on assumptions unacceptable to us, for instance, regarding the inferior status of women, the hereditary privileges of the priesthood, the desirability of sacrificial worship, the importance of ritual purity, the defiling effect of menstruation and the legitimacy in principle of capital and corporal punishment...

15

We cannot accord to the classical literary sources of the *halakhah* more than a presumptive authority, and therefore what they legislate needs to be weighed against the individual conscience, the needs and consensus of the community, and still other considerations including historical and scientific knowledge as relevant."[19] These are among the factors and considerations which a liberal Jew should critically weigh when deciding whether to observe a particular *mitzvah*.

7. Responsibility to the Covenant Community

Jakob J. Petuchowski claims that "Everything...which contributes to the survival and to the unity of the Covenant Community of Israel must be regarded as a religious commandment. Everything, on the other hand, which hurts the Covenant must be avoided. Bearing this perspective in mind, the Reform Jew will observe many a *mitzvah* toward which he might feel no personal obligation" because it is not "a matter of the individual only (but) also of the community as a whole." [19a]

According to this principle, our *pesikah* must take into consideration more than our own synagogue, community and movement. We must be aware of the ramifications of our *halakhic* decisions on *kelal yisrael*. When dealing with issues relating to marriage and personal status, to the physical and spiritual welfare of Jews outside of our community and to the relationship between Jews of the diaspora and Israel, we must be mindful of our being one people. In spite of diversification and severe conflict, we are all of us bound by that divinely contractual *berit* which our ancestors and we made with the God of Israel.

There is, of course, the possibility that some of these seven criteria may be mutually contradictory when applied to a specific situation. For example, this last criterion of responsibility to *kelal yisrael* may conflict with the principle of pluralism discussed above.

16

We shall have to rely on the wisdom and judgement of rabbinic scholars to determine which criteria, if any, are valid in each individual case. *Poskim* must exercise their judicial discretion wherever appropriate in accordance with the rabbinic dictum: "Everything depends on the judgement of rabbinic decisors." [20]

III. Progressive Principles in the Traditional *Halakhah*

The need for a framework of extra-halakic criteria to allow change has been questioned and even denied. Some scholars claim that all we have to do is to research the traditional halakhah where we can find a myriad of creative and even liberal principles which could enable progress in every generation. The following are but a few of the traditionally tested means of coping with changing reality.

When the sages of Alexandria decided to assign the status of *mamzerim* to children born of betrothed women (without a get) to other men, Hillel the Elder found a means of purifying these young people. He used the legal fiction of *doresh leshon hedyot*, giving a forced interpretation of a sentence in their *ketubot* (marriage contracts) claiming that these woman were not betrothed at all, so therefore their offspring were not *mamzerim*. [21]

In this context, almost every scholar makes note of Hillel's well known *prozbol* [22] and of the precept: *et laasot ladonai heferu toratekha,* which may allow the abrogation of a part of the Torah to save the whole. [23] We should emphasize an often neglected principle allowing creativity found in the Beth Hillel "Decree for the Repentant" which enabled a repentant thief to make compensation for a stolen house column that he built into his own home rather than fulfilling the Scriptural requirement of destroying his own dwelling and returning the original stolen object, as demanded by Beth Shammai. [24]

17

The universalist precept, *mipnei darkhei shalom* (for the sake of peace), was construed to include the obligation of visiting the sick of the gentiles, burying their dead and comforting their mourners.[25]

Another example of progress through creative *halakhic* action is R. Yehudah Hanassi's downgrading the sabbatical year from a Scriptural to a rabbinic commandment (*midoraita lederabanan*) which enabled agricultural work during the seventh year and thereby saved many from starvation.[26]

Proceeding to the Middle Ages, we might learn from Rabbi Moses Isserles (Ramah) who applied the Talmudic humanitarian principles of *kevod habriot* (human dignity)[27] and *shaat hadehak* (the necessity to act in an emergency situation)[28] to the problem of an orphan bride who was ready to enter the *hupah* in his Krakow synagogue on a Friday afternoon four hundred years ago. The families could not agree on the *nedunyah* (dowry) until after sunset and well into the Sabbath. Isserles was afraid that if he waited until after the Shabbat the *shiddukh* would irreparably fall apart and the orphaned bride would forever be shamed, so he married the couple in his synagogue on the Shabbat. The Rama explained that his action was prompted by this *shaat hadehak* - irreversible emergency situation - and the danger of injury to the human dignity of the unfortunate young lady.[29]

Many orthodox and non-orthodox scholars have searched rabbinic literature for similar principles to show the viable and vital character of the *halakhah* which enables it to adjust to changing times and conditions.[30] Many poskim in the distant past and even in recent generations were able to resolve difficult problems by exercising the flexibility and dynamism of the *halakhah*.

Indeed, this was the situation in the past. Notwithstanding this halakhic flexibility, our generation is still confronted with the

18

tragically unresolved problems of conversions made difficult or virtually impossible in many countries as well as the stumbling blocks of *halizah, mamzerim,* and other *menuai hitun* (unattached young Jews who are forbidden to marry their beloved) - all in the name of the halakhah! We have witnessed the obscurantism of some *poskim* in positions of political power who coerce non-Orthodox Jews in matters of personal statue. They often seem to be acting in accordance with the view of the Hatam Sofer that "anything new is forbidden in the Torah" and "the old and antiquated is always better."[31] Many have turned away from religious Judaism and from the synagogue believing that these phenomena represent the exclusive approach of the *halakhah.*

Therefore, it is incumbent upon us to make explicit the implicit principles of morality and humanism in Jewish law and apply them to the painful problems and tragic issues of our day and search for appropriate halakhic solutions. This is what I have attempted to do in exploring the above seven criteria of *pesikah,* which are but a few of many such essential principles.

***

Do these criteria constitute a radical departure from the spirit of our millennial tradition? On the contrary, I believe that these principles may indeed be the fulfillment of a significant trend in the philosophical and *halakhic* thought of our sages.

Joseph Albo, the great 15th century philosopher, asks in his *Sefer Haikarim,* why God did not spell out in his Torah the specific details of the *mitzvot* for all generations and in all circumstances. Should not the omniscient Creator have let us know in advance the solutions of all our *halakhic* problems from the religious status of women and men to medical transplants?

Albo proclaims: "On Sinai, Moses was given orally certain

general principles, only briefly alluded to in the Torah, by means of which the sages of each and every generation may work out the updated particulars applicable to their day."[32]

This may well serve as a challenge to the sages of our day who are called to apply the creative principles of *halakhah* to assuaging the pain of this troubled generation.[33]

1. Brief to the Supreme Court of Israel, High Court of Justice Case No. 47/82, 5784, Israel Movement for Progressive Judaism vs. Chief Rabbinate of Israel, *Chief Rabbinate Brief* p. 3, par. 8 and p. 5.

2. *Sifra* Behukotai, Leviticus 8:12.

3. Shabbat 104a

4. *J.* Peah 2:6

5. Menahot 29b

6. "Jewish Law: A Synthesis", *Conservative Judaism and Jewish Law*, ed. Seymour Siegel, New York, 1979, pp. 118-120.

7. Louis Jacobs, *A Tree of Life*, Oxford, 1984, pp. 239, 242.

8. Ibid., p. 245

9. Brief on behalf of IMPJ in above mentioned case (footnote no. 1) and my article, "The *Halakhah* in the View of Progressive Judaism," (Hebrew) *Shalhevet*, September, 1987 No. 34, pp. 4ff.

10. "A Dynamic *Halakhah*", *Judaism*, Spring, 1967, pp. 267ff.

11. *Tosefta* Yevamot 1:11 and parallels.

12. Eruvin 13b.

13. Ibid. 10b; Yitzhak D. Gilat, "The Formation of the *Halakhah*," *Hauma* 7:4, Iyyar, 5729, p. 455.

14. *Not in Heaven, The Nature and Function of Halakhah*, New York, 1983, p. 19.

15. "Ethics and the *Halakhah*," *Conservative Judaism and Jewish Law*, (note 6 above), pp. 125-126.

16. Cf. my articles "The *Halakhic* View of Destroying Homes" (Hebrew), *Haaretz*, 23 April, 1985; "Demolishing Homes in the West Bank and the *Halakhah*" in *Journal of Reform Judaism*, Spring 1986; "*Halakhah* and Occupation," *Jerusalem Post*, 20 May, 1988; and the chapter on "The Attitude to the Gentile Minority" in my forthcoming Hebrew book *The Sane Halakhah*.

17. *Dat Umada*, Jerusalem, 1955, pp. 272-275.

18. "The Builders," in *On Jewish Learning*, New York, 1965, pp. 72-92

19. From an unpublished lecture delivered at the Leo Baeck College, London, 24 June, 1985.

19a. *Heirs of the Pharisees*, New York, 1970, pp. 177-179.

20. Joseph Karo, *Beit Yosef Yoreh Deah*. 268 end, based on *Tosafot* to Yevamot 24b. This is related to the Talmudic principle "*Ein lo ladayyan ella mah she-einav ro'ot* (The judge must rely only on his own judgement) in Sanhedrin 6b Cf. Ben Zion Uziel, *Mishpatei Uziel*, Tel Aviv, 1935, part 1, Yoreh Deah, No. 14; Joel Roth, *The*

Halakhic Process, New York, 1986, pp. 83ff and Mark Washofsky's penetrating analysis in the following chapter.

21. Baba Matzia 104a, cf. *Tosefta* Ketubot 4:9 and *J.* Yevamot 15:3; see also Yitzhak D. Gilat, "The Interdependence of *Halakhah* and Reality" (Hebrew), *Studies in Cultural Educational and Social Problems*, Tel Aviv, vol. 4, 1972.

22. Gittin 26b

23. Berachot 63a; Rashi on Yoma 69a; Temurah 14b; See Eliezer Berkovits, *Halakhah, It's Power and Purpose* (Hebrew), Jerusalem, 1981, pp. 76ff.

24. Leviticus 5:23, Gittin 3:18.

25. Gittin 51a-51b, *Tosefta* Gittin 3:18.

26. Taanit 3:1, J. *Sheviit* 10:3; v. Y. Gilat, "The Influence of Reality on Halakhic Distinctions", *Molad*, 3, Sivan 5730, p. 285.

27. Berachot 19b

28. Shabbat 45a

29. *Responsa Haramah* (ed. A. Ziv), Jerusalem, 1971, No. 125, pp. 488-495. An English translation of this responsum is found in Solomon B. Freehof, *A Treasury of Responsa*, Philadelphia, 1962, pp. 113-117.

30. Among those who have developed this subject are Eliezer Berkovits, *op. cit.*, notes 14 and 23; Yitzhak Gilat, *Bar Ilan Annual* Ramat Gan 1970, pp. 117-132 and *op. cit.* notes 13 and 21; Louis Jacobs, *op.cit.* notes 6 and 7. This subject is further elaborated in my article in *Shalhevet*, *op.cit.* note 9 and in the chapter entitled:

"The *Halakhah* as a Developmental and Moral Phenomenon" in my forthcoming book. *op.cit.* note 16.

31. Moses Sofer, *Responsa Hatam Sofer*, Jerusalem, 1970 Orah Hayyim nos. 28 and 101, 181 and Yoreh Deah no. 9.

32. *Sefer Haikarim*, Philadelphia, 1930. ed. Isaac Husik, 3:23.

33. This chapter is based in part on my article "*Halakhah* Developmental and Pluralistic," *The Jewish Law Annual*, Boston, vol. VIII, 1989.

The Search for Liberal *Halakhah*

A Progress Report

Mark Washofsky

It is appropriate, at the inaugural conference of the Institute of Liberal *Halakhah*, to ask whether the concept of a "liberal *halakhah*" is anything more than a contradiction in terms. That is, can the system of rabbinic law accommodate contemporary values of justice, morality and progress? Is *halakhah* capable of the growth and development required to respond in a positive way to changing socio-cultural circumstances and ethical insights? Or does "liberality" suggest the translation (read: distortion) of Jewish religious law into a mechanism by which ethical values drawn from a secular culture may be draped with an appearance of sanctity? For some, it is an absurd notion that a legal system claiming divine origins can simultaneously "change with the times." There is, indeed, no shortage of thinkers on either the right or the left of the Jewish theological spectrum who deny the phenomenon of "creative change" in Jewish law. There are others, however, who view *halakhah* as dynamic and open to an affirmative encounter with modernity and its accompanying cultural transformations. These "liberals" are generally associated with liberal Jewish religious movements but are not restricted to them. Such "Orthodox" scholars as Emanuel Rachman and Irving Greenberg, for example, speak of the possibility of making directed changes, "within the frame and by its own methodology," in traditional Jewish civil, political, family and ritual law.[1]

In Israel, Effraim Urbach calls upon observant Jews to ensure "the revival of the *halakhah*" to its historic vitality and its adaptation to the needs of a modern state by wresting Jewish law from the control of "extremists" who reject both modernity and statehood. The structures and problems of modern life require that rabbis return to the activism that once characterized *halakhic* decision and adjust their methods of analysis to reflect changing economic and social reality.[2] Urbach and his colleagues, who writings fill the pages of *Amudim, Mahalkhim, De'ot* and other journals, deny that contemporary Orthodox extremism is synonymous with "*halakhic* Judaism."[3] While these groups and individuals differ in their sectarian attachments, they share the conviction that Jewish law can and must change to meet the challenges of our time, that *halakhah* is "much more open to diversity and to 'modern' sensibilities than the modern Orthodox myth is ready to acknowledge."[4]

The problem for these liberal *halakhists* - and indeed for our new Institute--is that this portrait of a dynamic and flexible *halakhah* is difficult to maintain in the face of concrete practice. Whether the *halakhah* can be or ever was "liberal", it is certainly not "liberal" today. The plight of the *agunah* and the *mamzer*; issues of conversion and Jewish status; the role of women in ritual and communal life; attitudes toward non-Jews and contact with them; questions of new technology and medical ethics; challenges to traditional Jewish life raised by the establishment of the state of Israel--these are but some of the areas in which *halakhah* has taken decidedly illiberal positions. Liberals contend that traditional rabbinic law can yield positive, "enlightened" solutions to these problems, and their suggested solutions have made up what might be termed the liberal *halakhic* agenda. Nevertheless, the vast majority of recognized *halakhic* authorities have invariably denounced these proposals as invalid. This yawning gap between theory and practice is the Achilles heel of liberal *halakhah*. One can hardly argue that there is no conflict between *halakhah* and liberal values when every suggestion for mending that apparent breach is rejected by the leading authorities as contrary to Jewish law.

26

It is customary to blame this rejection on a reactionary Orthodox rabbinate who intransigence stems from identifiable historical causes.[5] This, however, overlooks the essential theoretical objections raised by Orthodox *halakhists*, who contend that rabbinic law, as defined by its traditionally accepted criteria of validity, cannot sustain the innovations which the liberals suggest. If they are to prove their case, *halakhic* liberals must respond directly to these theoretical objections. It is not enough for them to claim that *halakhah* can be flexible; they must show that it is flexible *enough* to support the items on their *halakhic* agenda. This requires a detailed and precise theory of *halakhah* which will determine the criteria of *halakhic* legitimacy and demonstrate that the solutions advocated by today's liberals meet those criteria. As if to take up this challenge, three booklength studies of liberal *halakhic* theory have appeared during the past decade. Each author, in his own way, addresses himself to the criteria of legitimacy in *halakhah*: just what is it that determines whether a specific proposal is valid under rabbinic law? Taken together, these works constitute the present "state of the art" in liberal *halakhic* thought. This essay is an attempt at evaluation of those efforts. What have these scholars accomplished, and what remains to be done?

In *A Tree of Life: Diversity, Flexibility, and Creativity in Jewish Law,* [6] Louis Jacobs adopts an "historical" approach to liberal *halakhah*. This method offers much promise for the liberal *halakhist*, since the vast rabbinic-*halakhic* literature contains numerous instances of interpretation and legislation that display a heightened ethical consciousness and a sensitivity to the needs of the age.[7] The difficulty lies in basing a legal theory upon scattered cases, in proving that these reflect the rule rather than the exception in *halakhah*. To overcome this problem, Jacobs produces a thoroughgoing history of the post-Talmudic *halakhah*. The work, marked throughout by Jacobs' considerable Talmudic and theological erudition, is to date the most comprehensive such history ever published. His thesis is that *halakhah* is not an

27

exclusively academic enterprise; it takes shape within history and is thoroughly shaped *by* history. Jewish law "is influenced by the attitudes, conscious or unconscious, of its practitioners toward the wider demands and ideals of Judaism and by the social, economic, theological, and political conditions that occur when the ostensibly purely legal norms and methodology are developed." The *halakhic* decisions of rabbinic scholars are thus guided by "extra-*halakhic*" motivations that represent the scholars' interpretive understanding of "general Jewish values." Jacobs charts the variety of outside factors that have influenced *halakhah* through its history, showing how each of them - philosophy, mysticism, Hasidism, and encounter with the non-Jewish world - has left its mark on Jewish law. He describes in detail the adaptations made by the *halakhic* tradition to changing social needs, popular practice, and new technologies. Responding to these extra-*halakhic* influences, *poskim* have found ways to justify numerous innovations in the law. They have set aside Talmudic assumptions on human nature and behavior when subsequent observation has shown that these have changed. They have incorporated new conceptions of ethical conduct and good manners (*derekh eretz*) into the process of legal decision. While rabbis often describe this process as purely conceptual and theoretical in nature, history shows that Jewish law results from a dynamic interaction between Judaism's legal tradition and its highest ethical and spiritual ideals. Legitimacy, then, is to be found in the historical process: If Jewish law has always accommodated to change, there is no reason to suppose that such change cannot continue.[8] The rich detail provided by Jacobs proves beyond any reasonable doubt that *halakhah* has a history characterized by "diversity, flexibility, and creativity." It serves as well to support his contention that innovative and dynamic answers to the pressing problems on today's Jewish legal agenda[9] are fully in keeping with the spirit of the *halakhic* tradition.

It is questionable, however, whether any historical treatment, even one as extensive as *A Tree of Life*, is really helpful to contemporary *halakhists* who advocate specific solutions to these problems. *Halakhah*, like law, is a normative, rather than a historical discipline. An innovation in law is legitimate, not because lawyers have always made innovations, but because this innovation is justified by the criteria of validity recognized by the relevant legal system.[10] Historical factors which induce changes in a legal system are not to be confused with the internal rules that govern the system and its procedure.[11] That sages in the past have rendered decisions which can be seen as "liberal" does not by itself establish the *halakhic* validity of any particular innovation suggested to contemporary authorities. For example, that Jewish law has historically provided economic and social relief to women - the *ketubah*, the permit for the *agunah* to remarry through the relaxation of Toraitic rules of evidence, and the *takanot* of Rabbenu Gershom are examples which come readily to mind--does not mean that any measure undertaken to improve the status of women (e.g., annulment of marriage, inclusion of women in a *minyan*, their acceptance as witnesses) is *halakhically* legitimate. To win acceptance, each of these proposals must be justified through convincing *halakhic* argumentation rather than by appeal to the invisible hand of history.

The historian may respond that the notion of "criteria of *halakhic* legitimacy" is a fiction, a rationalization that hides the real motivation of the rabbinic judge. Jacobs, at the beginning of his book, assumes this position. The *halakhist*, he tells us (pp. 11-12), approaches a legal question by first determining the best answer according to his own understanding of Jewish "ideals"; he then searches for *halakhic* rules and principles - "acceptable legal ploys," Jacobs calls them - to support his opinion. This account of rabbinic reasoning is, of course, an anathema to Orthodox scholars.[12] Still, if Jacobs is correct in his reading of *halakhic* history, then any decision which is just and compassionate can, in the hands of a skillful textual scholar, be proven legally valid. Jacobs here is reminiscent of the "realist" school which once exerted much influence over American jurisprudence. Like Jacobs, the extremists among the "realists" downplayed the importance of legal rules, contending that judges begin with predetermined conclusions and move "backwards" to formal justification by means of the manipulation of the "paper" rules of law.[13] Legal realism in its extreme form is today considered *passé*; the dominant jurisprudential theories recognize that analytical reasoning places firm, objective limitations upon judicial discretion.[14]   Jacobs eventually admits as much with respect to rabbinic law. In an appendix, he considers the plight of the *mamzer*, the offspring of an incestuous or adulterous union whose status is "the most stubborn and embarrassing problem traditional Jewish law has to face" (p. 257). He concludes that this injustice cannot be remedied through textual interpretation. The traditional *halakhist*, no matter how liberal his sensibilities, is ultimately bound by loyalty to the sacred texts of the Jewish legal tradition. He may read these texts in a creative manner, but he is not free to ignore them or make them say what they manifestly do not say. Unlimited judicial discretion does not exist in *halakhah*. When the clash between liberal values and sacred texts is unavoidable, it is the texts that must prevail.

To solve such intractable problems, Jacobs calls for a "non-fundamentalist" *halakhah* which would combine tradition with the dynamism and flexibility that Jewish law has displayed through the ages.   While committed to the tradition, non-fundamentalist *halakhic* scholars would be willing to change the law, whether or not that change can be supported by the legal texts, whenever the existing *halakhah* leads to "the kind of injustice that reasonable persons would see as detrimental to Judaism" (p. 236). Jacobs thus abandons the attempt to demonstrate the legal validity of liberal *halakhic* innovations. It is not the text but the "higher values of Judaism" which establish the correctness of a decision. In this way,

30

he would insure that Jewish law would always conform to liberal values. The premium he pays for this insurance is the abandonment of the traditional legal system. His solution is of little help to liberal *halakhists* who seek to prove that justice and compassion can be achieved within the traditional *halakhah*.[15]

If the method of history cannot, on its own, establish a theory of liberal *halakhah*, the "analytical" approach offers a more promising solution. This approach characterizes the work of Eliezer Berkovits in *Hahalakhah: Kohah Vetafkidah*.[16] This is an analytical study concentrates not upon what rabbinic authorities have done in the past but upon the rules of the rabbinic legal process. Granted that changes have taken place, just what **is** it that makes these changes legitimate from a normative point of view? The analyst undertakes a "dogmatic" study of the law to determine the immanent procedures by which the particular legal system justifies its rulings.

Thus Berkovits, like Jacobs a *halakhist* as well as a theologian, does not follow Jacobs in drawing conclusions on the basis of historical circumstance. He also does not advocate a new, "non-fundamentalist" *halakhah*. The traditional *halakhah* is fully capable of securing justice and progress. As the eternal bridge upon which Torah traverses from abstract ideal to the concrete world of reality, *halakhah* can by its nature respond to the changing conditions of Jewish existence. This generation has experienced a more rapid rate of change than any other since the destruction of the Temple. Our time requires *halakhic* solutions to problems in all areas of religious and social life. It is imperative to show how this task can be accomplished within the traditional *halakhic* framework. In his first chapter, Berkovits argues that rabbinic law shows a marked preference for reason over arbitrary authority. He proceeds to discuss the principles by which the theoretical *halakhah* has made significant adjustments in light of *metsiut*, the realities of human nature and existence. There follows a consideration of the

31

ethical principles evoked by Talmudic authorities when calling upon individuals to go beyond the letter of the law and guide their conduct by a higher moral standard. The material is presented not as history but as *hiddushim*, novellae in the familiar *yeshiva* style. Berkovits cites historical examples, but his point is not merely to show that the rabbis have from time to time issued "progressive" rulings. The examples illustrate the underlying rules and principles, defining the extent to which the rabbis are empowered to depart from the traditional understandings of Jewish law.[17] Cases of rabbinic "liberality" are not coincidental. They are evidence of principles embedded in the fabric of *halakhah* which guide rabbinic decisions in concrete situations.

An example of such principles at work, to which Berkovits devotes considerable attention, lies in the area of marital law. Although normally a husband must issue a divorce of his own free will, in certain cases his consent may be obtained through coercion. In Ketubot 63a-b, we read of the wife who denies conjugal rights to her husband on the claim that he is repulsive to her (*mais alai*). Some authorities, notably Maimonides and Rashi, hold that this husband may be coerced into issuing a divorce. If the *halakhah* follows them, then the legal position of the wife, who cannot under Toraitic law divorce her husband, is dramatically improved. By moving out of the marital home and claiming "*mais alai*", she would set into motion a chain of events which would lead inexorably to her freedom to remarry. Especially in Israel, where government coercion may be employed against a husband who refuses to issue a *get* at the order of a rabbinic court, a remedy would exist for women who currently suffer as *agunot* because of the recalcitrance of their husbands. While most authorities reject the use of coercion in this instance, Berkovits concludes that "there is no solid Talmudic evidence against the position of Rashi and Rambam." [18] Since our ethical sense forbids us to force a woman to remain with a husband whom she detests, the rabbinic court may coerce the divorce if necessary. He reasons similarly on the question of rabbinic annulment of marriage.[19] While the sources dispute that question, he believes that the rabbis can indeed declare marriage null and void when the situation warrants such an extreme step. Morality demands that they utilize this power to improve the lot of the wife and protect her from exploitation.

Unlike Jacobs, Berkovits thus identifies the normative criteria of *halakhic* legitimacy. A proposed decision is valid in Jewish law 1) when it can be justified by source argumentation at least as plausible as that which supports other alternatives, and 2) when it expresses the principles of fairness and morality integral to the *halakhic* system. On this basis one may posit that the items on the liberal *halakhic* agenda fall within the parameters of legitimacy set by the internal processes of Jewish law. The only remaining question is whether today's rabbis are empowered to diverge from the rulings and interpretations of the sages of past generations and adopt new and innovative solutions. Berkovits argues that they are. Over fifty-eight pages of text, quoting extensively from classic comments of the *rishonim*, he constructs a theory of virtually limitless rabbinic discretion in *halakhic* judgement.[20] If a contemporary scholar, upon his honest reading of the sources and his estimation of the demands of the hour, determines that the *halakhah* must be understood differently than it has been understood in the past, he may rule accordingly. Even if the collective weight of legal tradition stands against him, "Jepthah in his generation is as Samuel in his own."[21]

Why then, if Berkovits is correct, does such discretion almost never happen? The *poskim*, in fact, seldom diverge from traditional understandings of Jewish law to create innovative solutions to *halakhic* problems. It seems that in exalting the freedom of the contemporary authority, Berkovits ignores the very real and powerful limit which historical consensus exercises over *halakhic* decision-making. The issue of coercion of divorce on the claim of *mais alai* is a case in point. The "lenient" opinion of Rashi and Rambam is rejected in no uncertain terms by R. Tam, Ramban, R. Shelomo b. Adret, R. Asher b. Yehiel,[22] R. Nissim Gerondi, R. Yitschak b. Sheshet Perfet and other luminaries, a rejection so complete that the position is not mentioned in the *Shulhan Arukh*. The commentators are in no doubt that the law here follows the consensus opinion,[23] and that opinion has never been challenged by subsequent authorities.[24] Thus, it is doubtful whether the rejected opinion is still an available alternative to the *halakhist*. What happens when a rabbi *does* challenge the historical consensus is illustrated by Berkovits himself. In 1966 he proposed his own *halakhic* innovation, a pre-nuptial stipulation agreed to by bride and groom that would annul the marriage in the event that the husband would one day arbitrarily refuse to issue his wife a divorce. This provoked a sharp response from R. Menachem Kasher, who contended that the Berkovits proposal did not overcome technical difficulties which had buried similar proposals in the past. Kasher's main point, however, was that Berkovits has no business contradicting the unequivocal ruling of the great *poskim* who prohibit the use of such a stipulation. During the course of the century a total of 1500 rabbis have explicitly rejected the institution of conditional marriage under any circumstances. The quality and quantity of this rabbinic opposition demonstrates that "there is no excuse to raise again a question which has already been examined and decided by all the sages of Israel. Their ruling must not be doubted."[25] Kasher expresses his scorn by never referring to Berkovits by name, but only as "a certain rabbi". Such is the fate of Jepthah when, even in the name of morality, he challenges the *halakhic* consensus.

This consensus, as understood by Kasher and by the leading *halakhic* scholars whom he cites, is not merely a tendency among rabbis toward extreme conservatism. It is presented as a working factor in *halakhic* theory, a principle that is recognized by the legal system itself and which places strict limitations upon the freedom and discretion which the *halakhist* enjoys. That is, proposed rabbinic decisions, no matter how extensive their Talmudic justification or how urgent their appeal to ethical necessity, are invalid when they run counter to the consensus opinion of the preponderance of *halakhic* authorities. It hardly needs emphasis that the innovations championed by liberal *halakhists* generally do contradict the consensus. One who wishes to argue for the *halakhic* validity of these suggestions must therefore prove that the contemporary rabbi may safely ignore the weight of consensus. Berkovits, it must be concluded, does not do this. His portrayal of a *halakhic* process in which rabbinic discretion is the rule is thoroughly one-sided. It explains neither the realities of *halakhic* practice nor the rabbis' own conception of how the system functions.

On the other hand, there exists a rabbinate which does conduct its *halakhic* business according to the Berkovits guidelines. The rabbis of the Conservative movement of North America have long declared their loyalty to the traditional *halakhah*. At the same time, speaking as individuals or through the Committee on Jewish Law and Standards of the Rabbinical Assembly, they have frequently taken stands which are totally at odds with the position of the *halakhic* consensus. In *The Halakhic Process: A Systemic Analysis*,[26] Joel Roth, a leading *halakhic* authority for the Conservative movement, sets out to prove that the legal decisions of his movement meet the criteria of validity recognized by rabbinic law. He therefore confronts the same theoretical problem which faces Berkovits: may the contemporary authority ignore or overrule the *halakhic* consensus?

Like Berkovits, Roth studies the immanent rules and procedures of *halakhah*. He differs, however, in his effort to explain *halakhah* as a system much like all other legal systems. He draws heavily upon the literature of modern jurisprudence, particularly the works of Hans Kelsen and John Salmond,[27] in helping to identify the "systemic" structure of rabbinic law. From Kelsen he adopts the notion of a *Grundnorm*, a postulated, pre-legal principle from which all other precepts of the legal system are derived. Such a concept exists in every system; in the *halakhic* system, the *Grundnorm* would read: "the document called the Torah embodies the word and will of God, which it behooves man to obey, and is, therefore, authoritative" (p. 9). Roth borrows Salmond's classification of all legal questions into questions of law and questions of fact, with the former divided into questions of law in the first sense (questions which the law has definitively answered) and questions of law in the second sense (questions as to what the law is). A question of law in the second sense is also a question of fact: that is, the judge must determine the true meaning of the words of a text, statute, or precedent. In the early stages of a legal system, most questions fall into this latter category. Over time, matters of uncertainty are gradually transposed into fixed, precise definitions and presumptions. Here the *halakhic* system differs from most others, since with the disappearance of the Sanhedrin there is no universally recognized body empowered to turn questions of fact into questions of law in the first sense. This implies a wider range of judicial discretion in *halakhah* than that existing in other systems. On all matters of legitimate *mahloket* - that is, "such that none of the positions can be legally demonstrated to be untenable or false" - the rabbinic arbiter remains free to exercise his discretion, even when an earlier authority has decided otherwise.

This discretion thrives in the *halakhah* even though a sense of the holiness of his task and of his inferiority compared with earlier scholars may deter the contemporary *halakhist* from rendering a decision "at variance with common practice or precedent." His freedom is guaranteed by the principle which Roth calls "the *sine qua non* of the system": *ein ladayan ela mah sheeinav ro-ot* ("a judge must be guided by what he sees"). Indeed, Roth calls this "the ultimate systemic principle" of the *halakhah,* the "systemic legitimization of judges to exercise judicial discretion as they deem appropriate." *Halakhah* does not recognize a doctrine of authoritative precedent; the rulings of earlier sages do not attain the status of *davar mishnah* (uncontrovertible legal presumptions) but may be challenged by later scholars who can support their viewpoint through source citation and reasoning.[28]

If judicial discretion enjoys the status of "systemic imperative" in rabbinic law, then there is simply no room for "consensus" as a working principle in *halakhah.* Consensus has a certain predictive value: if rabbis have always ruled in a certain way on a particular issue, it is probable that they will continue to do so. Nevertheless, this tendency to legal stability in no way restricts the discretion of later authorities to dissent from that ruling. The only limit upon rabbinic discretion in a system whose ultimate principle is *ein laayan ela mah sheeinav ro-ot* lies in the integrity of the *halakhic* authority himself. This implies that he conform to two demands. First, the potential *halakhic* authority must be characterized by *yirat hashem,* religious behavior indicative of his fundamental commitment to the system. That is, he accepts the *Grundnorm* as the reflection of God's word and will and recognized the rabbis as the sole legitimate interpreters of the *Grundnorm.* Second, the decisions of this authority must be supported according to the rules of *halakhic* reasoning and interpretation. These constitute the criteria of validity in Roth's "*halakhic* process"; any ruling meeting these criteria is, by definition, valid *halakhah.*

On this basis, the *halakhic* innovations of the Conservative rabbinate qualify for *halakhic* legitimacy. If, for example, a potential authority committed to the *halakhic* system should drive to synagogue on Shabbat, this highly unprecedented practice is valid *halakhah* so long as the authority believes it to be

37

"systemically defensible." His may be a minority view, but by the systemic rules of *halakhah* it must be recognized as a legitimate option. The same would apply to other Conservative *halakhic* innovations, such as the *kashrut* of wines and cheeses, the counting of women in a *minyan*, and the resort to conditional marriage. All of these positions are justified through traditional methods of *halakhic* argumentation and issued by rabbis committed to the *halakhic* system and its basic norm. All of them may therefore claim validity, even though they run counter to the consensus positions among the *poskim*.

Still, this theory of *halakhic* validity will not be persuasive to most *halakhists*. Despite his sophisticated explanation of *halakhah* as a legal system, Roth, like Berkovits, underestimates the power of the *halakhic* consensus as a working factor within that system. Consensus, a widespread agreement among *halakhic* scholars on points of law, is more than a guide to and prediction of future rabbinic decision. It is itself a "systemic" principle, a controlling mechanism that restricts the rabbinic discretion which, according to Roth, is the ultimate "systemic" principle in *halakhah*. Rabbinic decision-making, in this view, involves considerably more than the purely intellectual confrontation between the individual scholar and the authoritative text. The *halakhic* tradition is more than text. It contains as well that which R. Joseph Soloveitchik calls the "Massorah of conduct," the generally accepted modes of Jewish religious observance. The effect of this Massorah upon the understanding of *halakhah* is underscored by an Orthodox critic in his review of Roth's book. "Once a particular opinion has become normative for the entire Jewish community," he writes, "it becomes an integral part of the 'Massorah of conduct' which can no longer be changed on the basis of purely intellectual considerations." Rabbis loyal to *halakhah* as traditionally conceived would never violate this practical Massorah. Thus, they would never permit driving to synagogue and turning on lights on Shabbat, regardless of the textual justification that could be marshalled in defense of such rulings.[29] Liberal rabbis, who deviate from the 'Massorah of conduct' as defined by the preponderance of *halakhic* opinion, do not qualify as *halakhic* authorities; their writings, no matter how proficient in Talmudic analysis, are not to be regard as *halakhic* literature.[30]

Roth's theory, which attempts to explain the *halakhic* process while explaining away the *halakhic* consensus, is a conceptual model which explains how *halakhah* ought to work. Like other liberal approaches, however, it does not account for the way in which *halakhah* functions in the concrete world of rabbinic practice. For example, Roth's theory does not discuss the dominant role played by the *gedolei hador*, the leading *halakhic* authorities, in shaping *halakhic* practice. Unlike judges in a Kelsenian system, the *gedolim* are not selected through a rational procedure governed by systemic legal rules but by "a sure and subtle process which knows its leaders and places them in the forefront of a generation."[31] These men identify the *halakhic* consensus for their time and determine, in fact if not in theory, the parameters of legitimacy in *halakhic* argument.[32] To ignore their formal/informal function as a "Sanhedrin in exile" is to present an inaccurate picture of the *halakhic* system as it really is. Consider as well Roth's treatment of the phenomenon of codification in *halakhic* history. Since the writing of codes tends to limit the exercise of judicial discretion, he seeks to minimize the importance of codification by citing the remarks of well-known opponents of the *Mishneh Torah* and the *Shulkhan Arukh*. In theory, he has a point. Perhaps the views expressed by Ravad, Maharsha, the *Penei Yehoshua* and the *Sheelat Yaavetz* opposing the exclusive reliance upon codes *ought* to be seen as the "royal road" of *halakhic* practice. Yet this fervent theoretical wish is controverted by the fact that codes *have* been written; that they *have* been produced in response to a perceived need for legal clarity and certainty; and that these books *have* functioned to limit the scope of permitted decision-making. A more balanced view of *halakhic* history would have to place at least as much emphasis upon the factors which encourage codification as upon those which argue against it.[33]

If liberal theory holds that the *halakhic* consensus does not limit the freedom of the rabbinic judge, the *halakhic* facts are otherwise. Rabbinic discretion gives way to consensus, which operates as a working, "systemic" principle that cannot be explained away by means of theoretical construct. Indeed, it is difficult to imagine *halakhah* without such a principle. The Talmudic sources of Jewish law are an incredibly rich and varied treasury of rules, principles, custom and commentary from which almost any analogy can be made and almost any distinction can be drawn. Rabbinic lore recounts examples of sages who could declare reptiles to be kosher: i.e., they could offer rational, logical argumentation for every possible *halakhic* conclusion, including those which are obviously false. A religious legal system that values coherence and consistency could hardly survive if it permitted its scholars a largely unlimited discretion to rule on the basis of its classical sources. A controlling device that determines *which* analogies, distinctions and conclusions are the correct one to draw from the sources is thus a virtual necessity. In *halakhah* that control has been exercised primarily by two factors: 1) the use of "discretion," of creativity in reaching *halakhic* judgement, is restricted to the handful of outstanding scholar-saints of the generation; 2) the "correct" answer to a *halakhic* question is that which is accepted by the preponderant majority opinion among these sages.[34] *Halakhah*, in other words, is synonymous with the opinion of the *gedolim*, and the liberal innovations that run counter to the consensus view among them will be rejected as invalid. Any theoretical construct which ignores the very real power of this consensus is a description of something other than the *halakhah* as it operates in the real world. As long as the consensus stands unchallenged, no historical or analytical treatise can prove that *halakhah* is compatible with liberal values.

40

To return to our original question: Is there such a thing as a "liberal *halakhah*"? In order to answer in the affirmative, liberals need to advance beyond theory and to adopt a strategy of direct confrontation with the *halakhic* consensus. Granted that the consensus exists and that it functions as a "systemic principle" in *halakhah*, the task is now to show that the consensus position, when examined on its own terms, is intellectually weak and wanting. For example, utilizing accepted procedures of *halakhic* analysis, liberals may show that the viewpoint of the "preponderant rabbinic majority" is based upon poor reasoning, improbable analogies and misreadings of the Talmudic and *halakhic* sources. In other cases, where the consensus view is textually sound, analysis might reveal that the decision of the *gedolim* is no more than an arbitrary choice, and not necessarily the best one, from among a number of equally valid *halakhic* alternatives. Such an "inner critique" of rabbinic decisions would do much to strip the aura of inevitability from the consensus position. Indeed, if the observant community were to be made aware of the kinds of reasoning and argumentation that often support the consensus view, they might be less likely to grant it automatic recognition as *the* correct *halakhic* opinion.

This approach can be illustrated with examples culled from the realm of medical *halakhah*. We may begin with the question of abortion, which has become the subject of bitter controversy in the *halakhic* literature. Although liberals point to lenient opinions by various *poskim*, drawing upon solid support in the classical sources, concerning the warrant for abortion,[35] the emerging *halakhic* consensus restricts the procedure to cases of mortal danger to the mother. A major factor behind this conservative trend is the 1978 responsum by R. Moshe Feinstein. As the ruling of perhaps the preeminent *halakhic* authority of contemporary times, this opinion exerts an enormous influence upon Orthodox practice and the political activity of Orthodox organizations. Yet few Orthodox Jews

41

are aware of the processes of "reasoning" by which Feinstein reaches his conclusion. Confronted by important *halakhic* sources which support the opposing lenient position, Feinstein simply declares that those sources do not exist. The one, he claims, is a scribal error, the other a forgery.[36] This rabbinic *tour de force* brought a stinging rebuke from R. Eliezer Waldenberg, a leading champion of the more lenient view, who notes that to erase inconvenient evidence in such an arbitrary fashion is an unacceptable form of *halakhic* argumentation.[37] In considering the Feinstein-Waldenberg exchange, liberals might point out to all who are interested that even rabbinic giants are not immune from the occasional temptation to bend the basic standards of scholarly integrity until they break.

Indeed, Waldenberg himself does not enjoy such immunity; witness his responsum condemning the practice of in vitro fertilization (test-tube babies).[38] The *posek*, widely regarded as the leading authority on medical *halakhic* issues, bases his opposition largely on the grounds that the husband cannot fulfill the *mitzvah* of procreation through a child conceived in this manner. His argument is derived from the *Mishnah* in Kiddushin 69a, which declares the offspring of a Jewish father and a Gentile mother to be a Gentile. In an unprecedented interpretation of this passage, Waldenberg asserts that the reason that the child does not follow the father's status is that the conception occurred in an unnatural place, outside the womb of a Jewish woman, where no relationship is possible (*makom sheein hityahasut*). Since test-tube fertilization also takes place outside the womb of a Jewish woman, we must conclude that the child is not related to the semen donor. He does not stop there: it is also doubtful that this child is related to its mother. After all, Maimonides in *Moreh Nevukhim*, I, 72, holds that a human organ separated from the body ceases to be truly human; once the ovaries are removed, they no longer belong to the woman, and neither does the child conceived therein. This *gadol hador,* in other words, is willing to deny technological hope to infertile couples on the strength of a truly imaginative Talmudic interpretation and the scientific opinion of a twelfth-century philosophical work that is rarely cited in *halakhic* discourse. He goes on to cite what are undoubtedly the real reasons for his opposition to the procedure: the frightening potential for abuse, for science run amok, for a brave new world of genetic engineering. These fears are understandable, and we may share them. But where Waldenberg's social concerns are by far the stronger part of his responsum, his *halakhic* reasoning is weak, far-fetched and just plain bad. While it is true that the subjective judgments of the *posek* and his concern for the welfare of the community are integral parts of the process of rabbinic decision, it is intellectually dishonest to try to cover these motivations with a thin veneer of legal respectability.[39] By carefully distinguishing between legal and extra-legal concerns in the writings of the *gedolim,* liberals can help observant Jews identify cases where the decisions of those sages amount to no more than the translation of personal opinions and prejudices into the language of *halakhah.*

At times, the majority position, while textually sound, must give way to other viewpoints on grounds of reason and common sense. A case in point is the autopsy controversy, which continues to flare from time to time into the public consciousness. *Halakhah* is strictly opposed to routine autopsies, and the vast majority of *gedolim* also forbid autopsies upon the corpses of Jews for the purpose of medical education. Even here, the procedure is forbidden as a desecration of the corpse and the deriving of benefit from the dead.[40] Against the majority stands the ruling of R. Ben-Zion Uziel that autopsy for medical study involves the saving of life and cannot be construed as desecration, nor does medical education fall under the traditional definition of profit or benefit.[41] If, as usual, the *halakhah* here follows the majority, liberals would suggest that the victory of the consensus comes at a high cost. Listen to the kind of argument advanced in support of that position.

43

In response to concern that this ruling would render medical education impossible in *Eretz Yisrael*, Rav Kook suggested in 1931 that medical schools engage in the purchase and importation of gentile corpses for research. We should not worry, assures Kook, that this practice would inflame anti-Semitism. The Gentiles, at least the best among them, will recognize that "this nation, chosen to spread the light of holiness in the world...is entitled to a certain perquisite of holiness." While this statement merely insults the intelligence of its readers, it compares favorably to the position more recently enunciated by Dr. Yaakov Levy, who suggested that the science of pathology be left virtually in its entirety to the Gentiles, "whose world view does not insist that they show special reverence for their dead."[42] He demands, in other words, that the observant Jew adopt a stance of blatant moral hypocrisy: Jews may benefit from vital scientific information derived by Gentiles through procedures which Jewish law forbids as immoral. Such are the arguments raised on behalf of the opinion of the "preponderant rabbinic majority." It is certainly questionable whether many in the observant community could accept the reasoning and the value positions embedded in them. Liberals, for their part, would simply challenge observant Jews to confront these arguments and to consider whether, compared to the ruling of Uziel, the consensus view constitutes the best available interpretation of Jewish law.

These examples, along with others that could be cited, demonstrate that liberals can successfully challenge the *halakhic* consensus on "systemic" grounds. The notion that the opinion of the *gedolim* is the authoritative voice of *halakhah* rests, in the final analysis, on the presumption that this opinion is textually defensible, that it meets the objective standards by which the rightness of all rabbinic decisions must ultimately be judged. Even the *gedolim* do not claim to rule by the power of *takanah* or charisma. They claim rather that their authority derives from the sacred texts of the legal tradition and that their rulings constitute the best available interpretation of its literary sources. It follows that when these rulings are shown to be devoid of reasonable textual justification or founded upon arbitrary and debatable value choices, that authority disappears, and their decisions are no more "correct" than any other textually defensible interpretation of *halakhah*.

The ultimate goal of liberal *halakhic* writing is to encourage among the observant community an openness to alternative interpretations of law. Liberals cannot accomplish this objective by ignoring the *halakhic* consensus, a functioning and decisive element in the process of *halakhic* judgement. Still, we have seen that it *is* possible to refute the consensus by testing it against the criteria of validity recognized by all *halakhists*. Should they succeed in establishing such a refutation in a significant number of cases, liberals may well convince Jews who live by *halakhah* and take it seriously that there can be more than one "correct" answer to a *halakhic* question. Put differently, liberals seek to break the monopoly of the *gedolim* over *halakhic* decision. This ambitious goal will take much hard work. To challenge the consensus position over the broad range of legal issues will require the publication of books, articles, studies, reviews and responsa which by their quantity as well as quality will guarantee that liberal alternatives receive their fair share of attention in the marketplace of *halakhic* ideas. My hope is that our new Institute will contribute significantly to this end. In this way it will surely perform a vital and indispensable role in the continuing search for a liberal *halakhah*.

1. Emanuel Rackman, "A Challenge to Orthodoxy", *Judaism* 18, 1969, pp. 143-158; Irving Greenberg, "Jewish Values and the Changing American Ethic", *Tradition* 10, 1968, pp. 42-74.

2. Effraim Urbach, "Al Hachayat Ha-Halakha", *Publication of The Movement for Torah Judaism*, 2, Jerusalem 1968; reprinted in *Al Tziyonut Veyahadut*, Jerusalem, 1985, pp. 311-321. See also "Samkhut Ha-Halakha Biyameinu", *Al Tziyonut*, p. 330.

3. Perhaps to this list should be added the name of Haim David Halevy, the Chief Rabbi of Tel Aviv-Yafo, who has some interesting things to say about the "flexibility" of the *halakhah* to arrive at new answers to contemporary problems; *Aseh Lekha Rav*, 7, Tel Aviv, 1986, n. 54.

4. Peter J. Haas, "Responsa Reconsidered," *Journal of Reform Judaism*, XXX, 1983, p. 41.

5. Menachem Elon points to the loss of Jewish juridical autonomy at the beginning of the Emancipation period as the primary factor in Jewish law's loss of vitality; see *Hamishpat Haivri*, Jerusalem, 1978, pp. 73-74. Solomon B. Freehof traces Orthodox stringency to a reaction against widespread non-observance of ritual and civil law; see *Reform Responsa*, Cincinnati, 1960, pp. 3-12.

6. Louis Jacobs, *A Tree of Life*, Oxford, 1984.

7. See, for example, Robert Gordis, "A Dynamic Halakhah: Principles and Procedures of Jewish Law," *Judaism* 28, 1979, pp. 263-282, who cites the *prosbul*, the *heter iska*, and the *takanot* of Rabbenu Gershom among other examples.

8. An assumption which Gordis, p. 264, makes explicit.

9. Jacobs' version of that agenda (p.247): Women's rights, relations with non-Jews, issues concerning life in a technological society, the needs of the state of Israel.

10. See Novak, p. 6, and Joel Roth, "Halakhah and History," in Nina Beth Cardin and David Wolf Silverman, eds., *The Seminary at 100*, New York, 1987, p. 284. On "criteria of validity" see, in general, H. L. A. Hart, *The Concept of Law* Oxford, 1961, p. 92 and pp. 97-107, and Joseph Raz, *The Concept of a Legal System*, Oxford, 1970, pp. 95ff and pp. 107ff.

11. "The legal sources of law are authoritative, the historical (sources) are unauthoritative"; P. A. Fitzgerald, *Salmond on Jurisprudence*, London, 1966, p. 109.

12. See J. David Bleich, *Contemporary Halakhic Problems*, New York, 1977, p. XV.

13. See Hart, pp. 132-144. For a description of American legal realism, see G. Edward White, *The American Judicial Tradition*, New York, 1976, pp. 272 ff. The most succinct statement of the extremist position among the "realist" school is that of Jerome N. Frank, *Law and the Modern Mind*, New York, 1930. See p. 179: "all legal rules, principles, precepts, concepts, standards--all generalized statements of law--are fictions."

14. G. Edward White, "The Evolution of Reasoned Elaboration", 59 *Virginia Law Rev.* 279, 1973.

15. The difficulty is exacerbated by the connection Jacobs draws between his non-fundamentalist *halakhah* and the acceptance of higher Biblical criticism and modern theories of revelation (chapter 16). Since orthodox Jews would be unable to swallow these modernist theologies, Jacobs has in effect excluded them from participation in his new legal system.

16. Eliezer Berkovits, *Hahalakhah: Kohah Vetafkidah*, Jerusalem, 1981.

17. Examples of such principles: "the Torah was not given to the ministering angels"; *hora'at shaah*; *et laasot*; *lifnim mishurat hadin*; *veasita hayashar vehatov*.

18. Maimonides, *Yad, Hil. Ishut* 14:8; Rashi, *Ketubot* 63b, *s.v. la kayafinan la*; *Tosafot ad loc., s.v. aval*.

19. He refers the reader to his book, *Tenai Benisuin Uva Get* Jerusalem, 1966, where he discusses the issue at length.

20. *Hasagat Harabad, Yad* Hil. Mamrim 2:2, on the power of the contemporary beit din to annul a long-standing decree whose justification has disappeared; *Piskei Harosh*, Sanhedrin 4:6, on the right of the contemporary scholar to disagree with the opinion of the *geonim*; *Yad*, Introduction, on the fact that all post-Talmudic scholars are of equal legal 20.stature.

21. Rosh Hashanah 28b.

22. Berkovits submits *Responsa Harosh* 43:8 to a forced interpretation. The clear sense of that responsum agrees with the assessment of Asher's son, Yaakov, that his father rejects Rambam's ruling. See *Tur*, Even Haezer 77, fol. 116a.

23. For a list of authorities see *Beit Yosef*, Even Haezer 77, fol. 115b-116a. The "commentators" are *Magid Mishneh*, Ishut 14:8, *Helkat Mehokek*, Even Haezer 77, n. 5, and Biur Hagra, *Even Haezer* 77, n. 5.

24. R. Ovadyah Yosef, *Responsa Yabia Omer* III, Even Haezer 19, is an exception that proves the rule. R. Yosef does not suggest that the Maimonidean position is the "correct" one or that, on ethical grounds, it ought to be preferred over the consensus view. He permits coercion in a case of *mais alai* only because the couple in

question are Yemenites, whose community, by long-standing *takanah*, follows the rulings of Rambam in all cases. See, however, Shlomo Riskin, *Women and Jewish Divorce*, Hoboken, 1989.

25. R. Menachem M. Kasher, *"Beinyan Tenai Benisuin," Noam*, XII, 1969. For compendia of rabbinic opposition to earlier suggestions, see *Ein Tenai BeNisuin*, Vilna, 1930, concerning the 1907 proposal of the French rabbis, and *Ledor Acharon*, New York, 1937, on the proposal of the Rabbinical Assembly. In general, see Mark Washofsky, "The Recalcitrant Husband," *Jewish Law Annual*, IV, 1981, pp. 144-166.

26. Joel Roth, *The Halakhic Process: A Systemic Analysis*, New York, 1986. Roth is perhaps best known for his extensive and detailed halakhic justification for the rabbinic ordination of women and, generally, women's participation in the ritual and legal life of Judaism; see Simon Greenberg, ed., *The Ordination of Women as Rabbis*, New York, 1988, pp. 127-187.

27. Hans Kelsen, *The Pure Theory of Law*, transl. May Knight, Berkeley and Los Angeles, 1967; P. J. Fitzgerald, *Salmond on Jurisprudencey*, 12th ed. London, 1966.

28. See *Baba Batra* 130b-131a, and *Piskei Harosh*, Sanhedrin 4:6; Roth cites other *rishonim* as well. On precedent in rabbinic law see Elon, pp. 768-804, and Z. Warhaftig, *"Hatakdim Bamishpat Haivri"*, *Shenaton Hamishpat Haivri*, 6-7, 1979-80, pp. 105-132.

29. Walter S. Wurzburger, "The Conservative View of Halakhah is Non-Traditional", *Judaism*, LVIII, Summer, 1989, p. 378.

30. See Bleich, *Contemporary Halakhic Problems*, p. 78: "The deliberations and publications of the Rabbinical Assembly do not...properly come within the purview of a work devoted to Halakhah. Much is to be said in favor of simply ignoring

pronouncements with regard to Jewish law issued by those *who have placed themselves outside the pale of normative Judaism"* (emphasis added).

31. Emanuel Feldman, "Trends in the American Yeshivot: A Rejoinder", in R. Bulka, ed., *Dimensions of Orthodox Judaism*, New York, 1983, p. 334. This point suggests caution in attempting to explain *halakhah*, which is definitely not a "modern legal system", according to jurisprudential theories designed with such systems in mind.

32. Even a modern Orthodox critic of the *gedolim* bows to their *halakhic* authority; see Oscar Z. Fasman in Bulka, pp. 317-330.

33. See Menachem Elon in I. Eisner, ed., *Hagut Vehalakha*, Jerusalem, 1973, pp. 75-119. At the conclusion of his historical survey, Elon suggests that the needs of the hour require a new codification of Jewish law, thus drawing a very different lesson from halakhic history than does Roth. On the powerful tendencies among Sefardic and Oriental rabbis toward adherence to precedent and the virtual sanctification of the *Mishneh Torah* and the *Shulhan Arukh* in their legal practice, see Y. Z. Kahana, *Mehkarim Besifrut Hateshuvot* Jerusalam, 1973), pp. 8-88; Elon, *Hamishpat Haivri*, pp. 1139- 1144; and R. Ovadyah Yosef in Sefer Hayovel Lerav Yosef *Dov Halevy Soloveitchik*, Jerusalem, 1984, pp. 267-280.

34. See *Eruvin* 13b; *Sanhedrin* 17a-b and Meiri, *Beit Habehirah ad loc.*

35. See David M. Feldman, *Marital Relations, Birth Control and Abortion in Jewish Law* New York, 1975, pp. 268-294.

36. *Responsa Igrot Mosheh*, Hoshen Mishpat II, n. 69. The sources

mentioned are Tosafot, *Nidah* 44a-b, *s.v. ihu* (scribal error) and *Responsa Maharit*, n. 99 (forgery).

37. *Responsa Tzitz Eliezer*, XIV, n. 100.

38. *Responsa Tzitz Eliezer*, XV, n. 45.

39. On the role of subjectivity in rabbinic decision see Avraham Rabinowitz, *Techumin*, 2, 1981, pp. 504-512. The weakness of Waldenberg's legal argument is emphasized by the fact that R. Ovadyah Yosef permits in-vitro fertilization and regards the child as the offspring of its father and mother in all respects. See M. Drori in *Techumin*, I, 1980, pp. 287-288.

40. See the list of "*rov minyan verov binyan shel haposkim*" in A. S. Avraham, *Nishmat Avraham*, Yoreh Deah, p. 256.

41. *Responsa Mishpetei Uziel*, Yoreh Deah, n. 28.

42. Dr. Yaakov Levy in *Sefer Assya*, Jerusalem, 1, 1982, p. 207. Kook's responsum is found in *Responsa Dat Kohen*, n. 199. One can hear the sigh of relief emanating from these writings when they stress that autopsy is no longer as important in medical education as it used to be; see *Nishmat Avraham*, *loc. cit.*

Jewish Law: *Halakhah* and the Jewish State *

Haim Cohn

1.

For the purposes of this paper, "Jewish law" denotes the sum total of Jewish (ancient, medieval, modern) sources from which any legal norm or jurisprudential principle can be deduced. It is not confined to *halakhah*, that is, Jewish religious positive (or binding) law, nor to those parts of *halakhah* which would in legal parlance, be comprisable within the concept of "law" (as distinguished from morals, ethics, ritual etc.): *halakhah* is, in my conception, the part of "Jewish law" which was chosen to be religiously binding.

Believers in the divinity of Written and Oral Law are not disturbed by any jurisprudential questions of principle: the supra-human validity of it is not open to doubt or discussion, it is simply there, to be taken at its face value, to be "learnt," obeyed and revered. Principles or motivations underlying its norms are not subjects for human evaluation, even if they are legitimately (as by Maimonides) ascertainable. Nor do these norms lend themselves to comparison with any other legal system, because you cannot compare between divine and human law, or between truly divine and only pretentiously "divine" law. Historical and sociological data are irrelevant for understanding them - they are anyway timeless and immutable. They are by their very nature immune from criticism: they have only to be authoritatively laid down to be completely and unsurpassably perfect.

The agnostic legal historian (the "non-*halakhic* man", to paraphrase Rabbi Soloveitchik) is free to indulge in evaluations and comparisons - nay, he is under a moral and professional obligation to undertake them. He weighs the norms not only with regard to their utility and in the context of the circumstances and periods of their creation, but also in consideration of moral or legal principles on which they are based or which may be derived from them. He regards all Jewish law (including *halakhah*) as human achievement, produced by human agencies operating for human ends and in human spirit - including its "divinity."

Halakhah, that is, those norms which were clothed with binding force, is the product of choices, made imperative by the fact that you cannot possibly observe two or more contradictory rules at the same time or on the same subject. The choices which resulted in *halakhah* may have been authoritative and intended or pretended to be exclusive - but they are by no means the only possible choices. The unique greatness of talmudical law lies in the variety of possible solutions to a given legal or legislative problem; and we stand assured that those divergent propositions of law are all the words of One Living God- implying that God is not beyond contradicting Himself and that, under different circumstances and for different purposes, different laws may be devised or different constructions of the law may be legitimate (Erubin 13b). Not that the talmudic jurists indulged in the illusion, or sought to pretend, that their own propositions were no less, or perhaps even more, divinely inspired than those of their disputants. When the authenticity of divine tradition could be one of several optional tenets, the claim of one scholar for the authority of his version had as much justification as the claim of the other for the authority of a different version. It cannot even reasonably be assumed that in the course of the disputations recorded in the Talmud any of the eminent participants consciously rendered to himself an account of the divine mission in which he was engaged. The very disparity and multiplicity of actual or potential "Words of God" leave divine law, as it were, as a well nigh inexhaustible reservoir of various possible solutions to needs and problems as and when they would arise.

There is a difference in principle between choices made for normative or prescriptive and those made for contemplative and descriptive purposes. It would stand to reason that a normative choice should be of the least restrictive and most liberal proposition, thus avoiding unnecessary interference by the law in human liberties; or, at least, that the choice should be made on the merits of the competing propositions, weighing in each particular case the equity and justice respectively reflected by them, or, to paraphrase Kant, conditioning moral rules so as to make them into formal law. Neither of those methods was resorted to for the determination of *halakhic* norms. Exceptional cases are recorded in which *halakhah* was settled according to the better and more logical rationale given for the rule proposed by one of the scholars (e. g. Bekhorot 58a). Normally, however, the qualifications laid down for elevating a proposed rule to the rank of *halakhah* were formal and external - such as the majority rule, or the prevalence of certain scholars over others (in general or in particular areas of the law), of severe over lax laws, or of a norm that was acted upon, over one that was not - all technical aids to choose the more feasible or the more generally accepted law from among alternative proporsitions, but not the divinely inspired or willed law. In order to overcome the equally "divine" status of dissents not elevated to the rank of *halakhah*, such technical aids were themselves invested with a "divinity" of their own - not necessarily always with divine approval (as is so beautifully demonstrated in the famous dispute between Rabbi Eliezer and the majority over Achai's oven in B M 59b).

The chooser who has no normative purpose in mind is not confined to legal texts and is not in need of any such technical aids. He makes his choices from much more variegated sources. Our information of ancient law derives not only from law books: much of what we know of Greek law, for instance, comes to us from the poets and philosophers, not to speak of the orators. Our own biblical, apocryphal, talmudic, midrashic and medieval sources abound with non-legal matter, an important part of which (*agadah*) was *halakhically* excluded from the normatively relevant sources (*J* Peah 2:4). For the legal researcher they all are of immediate relevancy: customs, ideas, legends, hermeneutics, mystics - all subject only to chronology and etymology. The more so as most *agadic* story-tellers have participated also in legal or quasi-legal discussions, and their stories are apt to throw illuminating light on their and their contemporaries' customs, religious faith and legal reasoning.

What is true of hermeneutics is all the more true of the original biblical texts. It is not the law codes of the Bible that I am now concerned with, even the historical and prophetical books of the Bible are abundant mines of legal information. In fact, biblical history is a history of lawlessness (mostly, but not solely, idolatry), and it is no mere coincidence that all the prophets' upbraidings present us with grim pictures of laws disobeyed and of ineffective legal administration; and their ethical exhortations may serve as eloquent evidence both of the motivation of laws and of reformatory demands and tendencies.

Similarly, "Jewish law" is not confined to what would normally be regarded as within the purview of legislation proper, but extends to ritual and sacrificial law, to rules of bodily purity, and to norms which are essentially ethical or religious. Neither Written nor Oral Law differentiate between these types and classes of norms as to their legal status - such differentiations as there are (e.g. between *mideoraita* and *miderabbanan*) apply to all types and classes of laws alike. It has often been observed that from the point of view of Jewish law, the law cannot be divided into ceremonial and moral (as Spinoza did), and perpetuity or superiority be attributed to the latter (Moore II 7). But the question whether research into "Jewish law" can legitimately be confined to civil, criminal, administrative and such like branches of a modern system of law, does not really arise for the secularist: he does not regard himself bound by *halakhah* on any subject-matter, and he anyway draws his material from all available sources. For his purpose, it goes almost without saying that he will take his source material wherever he can find it, irrespective of its context and lack of actuality.

Like other phenomena of civilization, law is, more often than not, the result of acculturation processes. Its evaluation depends to a large extent upon how it compares with contemporaneous laws elsewhere. The chronology, systematics and dialectics of mutual or unilateral influences, of inseminations with ideas and principles, of imitations or adoptions of norms and customs, are eminent subjects of research. Jewish law has not only taken from, but also supplied to, other systems values and ideas and legal methods. Needless to say that it would in no way derogate from the value-content of a particular norm of Jewish law if its origin would be traced to non-Jewish law, nor would it add to such value-content if norms of Jewish origin were to be adopted elsewhere, the State of Israel included. We may even have recourse to foreign models and seek inspiration from non-Jewish sources, legal or philosophical, to better understand and evaluate matters of form, manners of conceptualization, and theories of law in Judaism.

But while methodolical and philosophical approaches valid for other ancient laws apply also to Jewish law, there is no denying its uniqueness. The great bulk of post-biblical law had neither for its creation nor for its enforcement the normal framework of statehood: it had to grow and develop often enough under alien oppression, almost in underground conditions. It bears the imprint of the exigencies of nomadism and migration, of deprivation and dejection, of self-righteousness in the desperate battle for self-preservation, and of an unabated repulsion from outside contacts and influences - small wonder that it also reflects the self-sufficiency born of seclusion and autoecism. That Jewish law could prosper and survive in such untoward circumstances is proof enough of its inherent vitality.

Such objective uniqueness of Jewish law is matched by a purely subjective assumption of uniqueness, which may not always lend itself to rationalizations. It consists in an emotional predilection for Jewish law, easily explained and, indeed, postulated in the case of those who believe in its divinity, but perhaps out of tune with the academic impartiality expected of the non-believer. Still, there is no denying its existence, and its disclosure may, in old legal fashion, perhaps cure some of its possible defects.

The Jewish national renaissance in Israel is not only a political but also a cultural phenomenon. The revival of the Hebrew language was not only a prelude to, but is a symbol of, the regenerative processes taking place in respect of Jewish cultural heritage as a whole. While modern Hebrew is very different indeed from biblical, talmudical and medieval Hebrew, its roots are the same, the grammar is the same, its spirit remained intact: it still is, and at the same time is no longer, the language in which God is said to have revealed Himself. In a similar vein, the history of Jewish civilization throughout the ages has now, as it were, assumed the character of contemporary history: our comprehension and understanding of it is induced by the requirement to maintain and develop a new civilization of our own (Croce 15). Much historical criticism must be involved in patterning this new civilization: nothing ought to be accepted at its face value and adopted only because it is there and handy. Historical reconstruction may lend the way to self-construction, when "patterns of the Jewish historical past become alive in the receiver, merge with his contemporary complexities, and emerge in a creative synthesis" (Fishbane).

Jewish legal history provides the Israeli student with a sense of continuity and identification, quite independently of the validity or desuetude and obsolescence of any particular norm. It is the motivations behind the normative or disputative pronouncements, or the principles underlying the enacted or rejected propositions, that preserved their actuality and their lustre throughout the ages. The foremost purpose of research into Jewish law is to discover those motivations and restate and analyze those principles. That some such motivations and principles may have undergone changes in the course of the centuries (as many of the norms themselves have changed), does not derogate from the potential validity of either the original or the subsequent ones. There is, of course, a temptation to lawyers to ascribe to ancient legal doctrines and institutions such like motivations as they had been brought up to expect of just and equitable modern laws; but it is the infusion of ancient law with contemporary ideology that qualifies it as living history.

As has aptly been said of ancient law in general, may also be said of Jewish law, that is, that the particular norms laid down in the books are but guidelines and signposts, never demarcation lines, of research, the norms are outward expressions or applications of legal ideas and may as such provide evidence of the legal consciousness of the time in which they were created. Looking at particular norms, then, symptomatically, they will divest themselves of their dogmatic character as commands or prohibitions and assume the character of elements, qualities and functions of legal institutions and principles (Ihering vol. I, p. 3).

The description of legal norms that are no longer (or never were) binding, "would be comparatively useless and uninstructive, unless explained and justified, and that in every title, by a continued accompaniment, a perpetual commentary, of reasons, of rationale" (Bentham). Our childhood familiarity with terms and

59

norms may well lead to a fallacious assumption of the facility of the matter. Where the rationale is expressly given in the texts (as distinguished from commentaries and glosses), it will only have to be restated, classified, systematized and chronologized; it is where the rationale is not so spelt out that the researcher must probe into and analyze all possible constituent ideas, underlying causes and legal and sociological sources and precedents. In the vast majority of cases, a rationale, or several divergent ones, were superimposed on the norm, often changing the norm in the process; such rationale will then, in its own right, become the subject-matter of research. The fact that the norm, in its original or final form, is not (or never was) binding, is as irrelevant to this enquiry as is the binding or non-binding character of the rationale.

If talmudical precedents were needed, it is well known that the sages already indulged in the exercise of reducing norms to principles (Makkot 24a). We are told that the 613 commandments of the Written law were reduced by King David to eleven, by Isaiah to six, by Micah to three, and by Amos and Habakuk to one - and it is significant enough that all those reduced principles are ethical in nature. Rashi's explanation that the number of commandments had to be reduced because of the deterioration of the generations, seems to indicate that however much the generations would deteriorate, the ethical part of law was to be and could be observed in all ages and by all people. The same notion underlies Hillel's famous dictum to the effect that the whole of God's law is a fundamental principle of human ethics - everything else you can go and look up (Shabbat 31a). We go and look up everything: but the right method to explore and expound the law is to grasp its essence.

2.

When the State of Israel was to be established, it was generally expected, as a matter of course, that Jewish law would, in the Jewish state, replace Ottoman and British laws. This expectation was oriented on three different assumptions: such orthodox people as aspired to a new theocracy, wanted *halakhah*, in its own right, to govern the state (and, of course, all its citizens); uninformed Zionists, who had no idea of what Jewish law really was, wanted it because it was "Jewish" and hence sufficiently qualified; lawyers and others who know something of Jewish law and were afraid of its antiquity or of its religious connotations, wanted Jewish law to be modernized and adapted to the needs of a liberal and progressive democracy, before it could - as it should - be made the law of the land.

None of these "orientations" stood the test of time and politics. Israel became a democracy, not a theocracy, and Ben Gurion proclaimed it to be "a state ruled by law, not by *halakhah*". There originally was a great majority supporting the idea of modernizing Jewish law so as to render it fit for reception; but the enthusiastic efforts at writing a new and modern code of Jewish law were brought to nought by the vociferous opposition of the orthodox whose political parties had meanwhile gained a position of (bargaining) power. Their argument was (and is) that no secular legislature could presume either to enact or to change or to repeal divine law, and that any "modernization" of Jewish law, otherwise than by virtue of *halakhic* authority, would be a trespass on divine prerogatives. There the matter rested - nothing being farther from the intention of the legislature than to commit so unholy a trespass.

As far as marriage and divorce are concerned, the secular law provides them to be governed by the respective personal laws of the parties, that is, for Jews by *din torah*. It was never disputed that *din torah* comprises the whole of *halakhah*. To the limited extent that *din torah* applies, *halakhah* has become an integral part of the laws of Israel: outside the realm of marriage and divorce, Jewish law does not come within the statutory definition of "law",

61

and has not been invested by the legislature with any binding force, or any standing at all.

But even in the realm of marriage and divorce, Jewish law is in no other and no better position than Sharia law is for Muslims and Canonical law for Christians, in other words, the hegemony of *din torah* in these matters is not a tribute to, or distinction of, Jewish law as such, but is only an incidental result of a long-standing legislative policy which Israel has continued but not initiated. But whatever the political legitimation, and the lack of prospect of political change, the law of marriage and divorce in Israel provides a shocking illustration of the calamities and injustices caused by the (more or less) mechanical application of formal *halakhic* norms and the discardment of principles or motivations underlying them.

Take the *halitzah*: Biblical law (as some other ancient laws) provides that a childless widow has the right to a levirate marriage, and that her brother-in-law (*yavam*) has the duty to marry her, so that the name of the deceased may not by "blotted out" but be borne by the first child born to them. The purpose of this provision is, as the text states, the fictional perpetuation of the deceased's lineage; but it is manifestly also that the childless widow, who lives in the parental home of her husband by virtue only of his title or that of his heirs born by her, should be protected from being thrown out. If the *yavam* refuses to perform his legal duty, the widow has the right to sue him before "the elders of the gate" who "shall then summon him and talk to him. If he insists, saying, I do not choose to marry her, his brother's widow shall go up to him in the presence of the elders, pull the sandal off his foot, spit in his face, and make this declaration: Thus shall be done to the man who will not build up his brother's house" (Deut. 25:7-9). I have set out the text in order to show that this unsandalling (*halitzah*) is the sanction which the law provides for the refusal on the part of the *yavam* to enter into the levirate marriage, and that this sanction cannot (and will not) be imposed upon him unless the widow so demands (it seems that such unsandalling and spitting was a public insult and humiliation severe enough to deter a prospective *yavam* from refusing , and that upon refusal this insult and humiliation was regarded as punishment enough). Failing the explicit complaint of the widow, nothing happens to the obstinate *yavam* - but the widow presumably loses her right to stay with her husband's family, and that is her cause of action against him. In order to survive and have a roof over her head, she must find herself a "stranger" for her husband (Deut. 25:5). But the introductory words in the biblical text, according to which the "shall not be married to a stranger outside her family," were interpreted by the sages to prohibit her remarriage, even where she had been perfectly willing to enter into the levirate marriage and perpetuate her deceased husband's name. This interpretation resulted in a new *mitzvah* being created: it was no longer the right, but became the duty, of the widow to unshoe her brother-in-law and spit in his face, failing which she would not be allowed to remarry; and soon enough the law was settled that this *mitzvat halitzah* took precedence over *mitzvat hayibum*, that is, over the divinely ordained levirate - if only because the sages had very good reason to apprehend that a willing brother-in-law might desire his brother's widow not just for the purpose of honoring his memory (M. Bekhorot 1:7, Yebamot 39b). The prohibition to be remarried to a "stranger" was originally intended to punish the widow for her refusal to enter into the levirate marriage; now she is punished only for the refusal of her brother-in-law to let himself be unshoed and spat at. The divine purpose of protecting the widow has been frustrated: instead of being protected, she is now exposed to the whims and blackmailings of her brother-in-law who is, by refusing *halitzah*, in a position to prevent her remarriage; but even if (and when) he consents, she and he are, by virtue of Jewish law, subjected to the humiliation and ignominy of a meaningless rite which borders on the outrageous.

The divine bias in favor of widows (to use an expression of Reinhold Niebuhr) is attested to in unmistakable terms, and time and again was impressed on obstinate judges from the mouths of the prophets (Ex. 22:21, Deut 10:18, e.g. K. 1:17,20). It is as if no cognizance is taken of it in "Jewish" law: in this respect, our rabbinical courts are not better than were the judges who were denunciated by the prophets. Not only has formal law (wrongly interpreted) been allowed to supersede and almost obliterate fundamental principles, but it has, to a large extent, contributed to the disrepute in which Jewish law has fallen in Israel.Examples of this kind of anachronisms and injustices in the Jewish law of marriage and divorce can be multiplied.

At least from the point of view of principle, a much more felicitous attempt to introduce Jewish law was made in 1980 with the Foundations of Law Act. The Act was intended to abolish the resort to English common law as a "residuary" law, that is, to fill any lacuna or gap arising when no other law (including custom and precedent) could apply to the matter in issue. It is now provided that instead of resorting to English law, courts will in such cases have to resort to "the principles of liberty, justice, equity and peace, of the heritage of Israel". Significantly enough, there is no reference here to *halakhah* or *din torah* or Jewish law: what is meant by "the heritage of Israel" will in due course have to be determined by judicial interpretation. I have elsewhere suspected that this "heritage" is not confined to either *halakhah*, *din torah* or Jewish law; but be that as it may, the legislature made it very clear that what can be applicable are only "principles", and from among the principles only those that proclaim and vouchsafe liberty, justice, equity or peace. I submit that this is the right approach to the application of Jewish law in general: what we can and should adopt are principles, not formal norms; and we must be autonomous in our choices and selections, and not let us be led astray by the "Jewishness" of what we regard as injustice. Within the framework of the 1980 Act, the choices are to be made by the judge to fit the particular case before him; the only reason why such like choices of lofty principles should not be elevated to the rank of general legislative policy, is that orthodox and secular parties will be, and always remain, hopelessly divided as to what these principles actually are, and even where to look for them.

Apart from marriage and divorce and this residuary law, Jewish law (or heritage) as such has never been enacted by the Israeli legislature. Some scholars have probed into the various acts of the legislature with a view of ascertaining whether and to what extent they conformed to or deviated from corresponding rules of Jewish law: When they have found some provision to be conforming, they rejoiced in the discovery that Jewish law had been adopted; when they found it unconformable, they lamented the disregard of Jewish law. This kind of investigation is irrelevant and misleading. Whenever the Israeli legislature enacted a rule the like of which can be traced in Jewish law, it was either on its actual merits, regardless of its origins or parallels, or on internal political pressure or extortion, regardless of its merits or demerits.

A good example for legislation on its merits is provided by the Surety Act of 1967, whereby "the surety and the debtor are jointly and severally liable to the creditor, but the creditor may not require of the surety any payment without first requiring the debtor to discharge his debt." This means that the creditor must first give notice to and make demand on the principal debtor, but he need not take proceedings against the debtor first: He may sue the debtor and the surety jointly or any one of them separately. This provision is said to be contrary to Jewish law under which the creditor may not proceed against the surety unless and until he had sued the principal debtor and the judgement against him had remained unsatisfied (B. B. 173b). While protagonists of Jewish law urged the legislature to adopt the talmudic rule, the legislature did not do so, not from any motive concerning Jewish law, but

65

solely in consideration of the merits. In support of the plea for adoption of the talmudic rule it was asserted that the principle underlying it was logically and equitably superior to the alternative (Elon) - an assertion which apparently did not commend itself to the legislature.

On the other hand, the Bailees Act, also of 1967, introduces the distinctions between *shomer hinam*, *shomer sahar* and *shoel*, of talmudic parentage, and then allots to each of them the liabilities respectively attaching to them, more or less - but not exactly - corresponding to the rules of Jewish law. It is true that during parliamentary debates several members expressed satisfaction that both terminology and substance of the law originated in our ancient sources; but even here the similarity between the legislative act and Jewish law is purely incidental, arising not from any predilection for Jewish law as such, but solely from the merits of the respective rules.

But even in those (rare) cases in which the legislature intended and purported to enact Jewish law, *halakhic* rules had to give way to present-day requirements. Take the Law of Return: When the Orthodox parties had succeeded to have the *halakhic* definition of a "Jew" incorporated in the law ("A Jew is a person born of a Jewish mother or converted to Judaism and who does not belong to another religion"), the Knesset proceeded to confer the rights of Return - which were to be the privileges of Jews - also to certain non-Jews, namely the non-Jewish children and grandchildren as well as non-Jewish spouses of a Jew. These non-Jews who did not and need not convert to Judaism, enjoy the rights of Return whether or not the Jew related to them was dead or alive, and whether or not he or she had ever come to or had any other connection with Israel. On the one hand, the legislature contrived to leave the Jewish law definition of "Jew" intact and adopt it almost *expressis verbis*, in express terms and this time not because of its merits, but solely because of its being Jewish; on the

66

other hand, the lawgiver prevented the harm and hardship which that definition may have caused by the disruption of mixed marriages and the splitting of family ties. Or, the legislature's interest in encouraging the Return also of Jews who had intermarried, and of their next of kin, prevailed over any *halakhic* exclusiveness. And in the long-raging storm over the validity of non-orthodox conversions, the legislature could not (as yet) be moved to adopt the formula "according to *halakhah*", notwithstanding the heavy political pressure brought upon it.

Then, it is claimed, a reception of Jewish law has taken place in what is known as *hakikah datit*, that is, legislation in the field of Jewish religious practices. Laws providing for *shabbat* and Jewish holidays to be official days of rest, or for *kashrut* in Army kitchens and canteens, or for the prohibition of raising pig, or for the restriction and control of post-mortem examinations, or for exemptions from army service, or making the display of *hametz* on *pessah* a criminal offence - have all been said to incorporate Jewish law by implication. In fact, none of them does. There is a fundamental distinction between reception of another law (like Jewish law) as such and the reception only of the pur pose for which also other laws have been made: it is true that by enacting religiously orientated laws the legislature lends its hand to serve some purpose of the Jewish religion; but this does not mean that it incorporates Jewish law even in regard to those purposes. Declaring Shabbat to be the official weekly day of rest is one thing; but adopting minutiae of *halakhah* as to the manner in which Shabbat is to be observed, is quite a different thing. What we adopt is the divine principle of resting one day each week, and Saturday is the natural and traditional day on which to rest; not the ancient rules as to how this rest ought to be carried out. The prohibition of raising pig was certainly intended to promote observance of the religious commandment; but then the prohibition of biblical law relates to eating pork, and it is exactly this particular

67

prohibition which the legislature advisedly refrained from enacting (Lev. 11:8). The same applies to the prohibition of displaying *hametz* on *pesah*: the prohibition of the biblical law is that no *hametz* may be kept in one's possession, not just that it may not be displayed to the public. And as for the exemption of girls from Army service, one would have thought that if there were any such provision in Jewish law which could have been adopted, it would surely have to be applied not only to religious girls; in fact, it is good Jewish law that (at least in wars of defense, *milhamot mitzvah*) it was the duty not only of men but also of women to enlist and fight (*M* Sota 8:7).

As in matters of religious ritual, so in matters touching upon religious general precepts, the question of applicability of Jewish law was raised time and again. When in a bill providing for the mutual rights and duties of parents and children it was proposed to insert a clause to the effect that it was the duty of a child to honor and obey his or her parents, objection was made on the part of the orthodox for the reason that incorporation of a Decalogian law in secular legislation would not ensure its observance but only derogate from its sanctity. The objection did not prevail; if it had, prohibitions of murder and theft might also qualify as divine law not be desecrated by secular impurity.

Conversely, when the Knesset - over much objection from the left - re-enacted a British statute providing for imprisonment for civil debts, protagonists of Jewish law maintained that this enactment "represents a complete adoption of the Jewish law in this matter as it finally took shape" (Elon). The emphasis is on the last words, because originally imprisonment for debt had expressly been denounced as contrary to the letter and spirit of Jewish law (Maimonides *Hil. Malveh*, 2:1).

Or, when the legislature fixed the minimum marriage age for girls at seventeen, one would think that was a radical deviation from original Jewish law by which girls were allowed to marry at the age of twelve years, six months and one day (Kidd. 79a, Maimonides *Hil. Ishut* 2:1-2). But as the Knesset refrained from nullifying child marriages and contented itself with penal sanctions, the law was acclaimed to be pursuant to Jewish law, the more so as the Chief Rabbinate had some time earlier issued a direction to the effect that marriages should not be performed of girls below the age of sixteen.

Again, when the Succession Act of 1965 provided for maintenance out of the estate for persons who had been dependent on the deceased for their livelihood and had no other means of living, especially where they were disinherited, this provision was hailed as originating from Jewish law. But the maintenance of widows and daughters is in Jewish law provided to them in lieu of their shares in the inheritance; and where they inherit (by law or by will), they have no claim to maintenance. Not only insofar as positive law is concerned, but also in respect of underlying concepts and principles, the Israeli law of maintenance out of the estate has really nothing in common with Jewish law except the name only.

Finally, there are some legislative acts which may be said to refer to Jewish law by necessary implication. When the State Education Act of 1953 speaks of "religious education" and the "religious way of life", reference must, of course, be made to religious law to ascertain their meanings. (A government Council for Religious State Education is charged with finding those meanings out.) Or, the duties to be performed by Religious Councils under the Jewish Religious Services Acts, such as *shehitah*, require for their implementation the resort to the pertinent *halakhic* rules. Or again, under the Evidence Act of 1971 a minister of religion is entitled to withhold evidence entrusted to him in confidence, if by "the laws of his religion" he is prohibited from disclosing it. It falls to the respective religious laws to decide who is a "minister" and what rules of secrecy bind him. Curiously enough, this confidential privilege was also claimed by some rabbis as vouchsafed to them by Jewish religious law.

3.

Apart from the application (or, rather non-application) of Jewish law in Israeli legislation, there is the always recurring question of its application as yardstick or guideline for judicial determinations. We have already seen that in cases of lacunae, the principles of liberty, justice, equity and peace, of Jewish heritage, are applicable by statute; but what about the judicial interpretation of Israeli law where there is no lacuna? If an act of the legislature is interpreted by the courts by referring and resorting to Jewish law, this would - in good legal theory - mean that such reliance may or must have been in the intention of the legislator for the construction of his act. In other words: courts will not, except by way of obiter dicta (i.e. incidentally, by way of gratuitous addendum), construe a statute by reference to Jewish law, unless it must or may be assumed that the legislator intended Jewish law to be the proper channel of interpretation. The reason for such an assumption can legitimately lie in any of the following five situations only, namely: first, when the resort to Jewish law is expressly prescribed or must necessarily be implied; second, where the legislators used terminology derived from Jewish law; third, where the substance of the statutory rule was or could have been derived from Jewish law; fourth, where the purpose of an enactment was a purpose of Jewish religious practice; and fifth, and most important, where the matter falls within the discretion of the judge to be decided according to justice or public policy or such like general or ethical considerations for which recourse can be had to principles of Jewish law. I shall give a few examples from decided cases to illustrate each of these categories.

70

First: In matters of marriages and divorces of Jews in Israel, including matters of maintenance or questions incidentally arising in other causes, the civil courts, too, and not only rabbinical courts, are by explicit legislation required to apply Jewish law (*din torah*). When long ago (1951) the question first arose as to whether a civil marriage contracted abroad without *hupah* and *kidushin* could be held valid in Israel, notwithstanding the applicability of Jewish law under which such a marriage was null and void, the court held that any application of Jewish law was subject to the rules of private international law, and that a marriage which was valid at the place of celebration would be recognized as valid in Israel. The court conceded that rabbinical (and other religious) courts need take no cognizance of private international law - with the result that the same marriage could be held valid in a civil and invalid in a rabbinical court. The same rule applies to mixed marriages: while invalid under Jewish law, they are held valid by the civil courts if valid according to the law of the country where the marriage was contracted. On the other hand, if the marriage contracted abroad was valid according to Jewish law but invalid according to local law, as e.g. *hupah* and *kiddushin* without the prescribed marriage license or registration, it would be held valid here even by the civil court, *ut res magis valeat*, to validate and not to invalidate.

A ticklish question arose as to whether civil courts were bound by the determination of Jewish law by the rabbinical courts: in a case in which a civil court must apply Jewish law, when rabbinical courts have already decided identical or similar cases, has the rabbinical ruling any precedential authority? The Supreme Court was divided on this question: according to one opinion, as the Court was not bound by its own or any other precedent, it could not be bound by decisions of rabbinical courts and had to lay down the law (including the Jewish law applicable) to the best of its own knowledge and discretion; according to the other opinion, rabbinical courts being recognized as authorities on and experts of

71

Jewish law, the Supreme Court will - if only out of comity - always bow to their superior knowledge and expertise. It would, indeed, be absurd for a civil court to prefer a ruling of the Rashba, for instance, where the rabbinical court had ruled to prefer the view of Rivash. However, where the civil court had to make a choice between contradictory rabbinical rulings, the most liberal and equitable solution would be taken where it could be found: "why should we not follow eminent *poskim* like Maharam Rotenburg, even when later authorities had decided otherwise." Rabbinical courts would probably have followed the latter (*halakhah kabatrai*) and conflicting decisions might result.

Second: Where the legislature, albeit in wholly neutral secular legislation, uses terminology manifestly taken from sources of Jewish law, the courts may have recourse to Jewish law for interpreting the meaning of such terms. The law reports abound with cases in which legal terms were so interpreted, or were advisedly refused to be so interpreted - terms like *garam, gemirat daat, habbala, hanina, hezeik, musak, ones, oshek, reshut, shekhiv mera, toshav,* to quote just a few. Sometimes the court is prompted by argument of counsel that the term in issue should not bear its popular or natural meaning, but should be given the meaning attached to it in Jewish law; more often the court acts on its own initiative, especially where a term lends itself to several possible interpretations. Not every reference to Jewish law results in its application: it sometimes happens that the interpretation according to Jewish law might result in hardship or injustice; in such a case it will unhesitatingly be discarded in favor of some other - possibly the court's own - interpretation which is found more equitable or more in line with the particular legislative purpose. It may also happen that of several different meanings which were attached to a given term at different times or by different scholars and judges, the court chooses not necessarily the one which was elevated to the rank of *halakhah*, but the one commending itself as the best suited for the purpose at hand. Or, the very fact that there were differences of opinion about the meaning of a term, would be sufficient to adopt any of such meanings. Take Mammon, for instance: the *halakhah* was settled to the effect that *mamon* did not include non-tangible benefits; but the talmudic discussion about whether it should or should not include them, was justification enough to adopt the non-*halakhic* meaning (Kid. 58 a-b et al.).

Third: The jurisdiction of rabbinical courts in matters of marriage and divorce is conditional on both parties being "Jews". Where the rabbinical court found a party to be *safek yehudi*, that is, entertained doubt as to his or her being Jewish, the Supreme Court issued a writ of prohibition, a *safek yehudi* not being included in the category of "Jew" (and a statute depriving ordinary courts of jurisdiction and vesting such jurisdiction in special tribunals, having to be construed strictly). Conversely, where a party claimed to be a Jew subject to rabbinical jurisdiction and the rabbinical court denied him access, the Supreme Court enquired into the question whether that party (a *falasha*) was or was not to be regarded as a Jew under Jewish law.

To determine the extent of the power vested in the Chief Rabbis to allow bigamous marriages, or the extent of powers vested in central and local rabbinates to control *shehitah* and *kashrut*, the Supreme Court probed into purely (or allegedly) *halakhic* considerations of the rabbis in order to find out whether they were within their statutory powers.

Although non-conformity with fundamental principles of natural justice by religious courts is regarded as an excess of their jurisdiction, the irrebuttable presumption being that any jurisdiction conferred by the legislature is conferred on the implicit condition that it be exercised only in conformity with natural justice - the Court took pains to show that the same principles of natural justice obtained also in Jewish law and that disregarding them amounted not only to an excess of statutory jurisdiction but also to a violation of Jewish law.

It is Israeli statutory law that in matters concerning minor children, the welfare of the children must always be the paramount consideration. It has been asserted that the same principle obtained also in Jewish law; but then, in Jewish law, the rule allegedly based on this principle is that girls of all ages are to be in the mother's custody, and boys over six years of age in the father's custody (Ket. 65b, 102b,). It is a duty incumbent upon fathers to teach their sons *torah*, whereas mothers and daughters are exempt both from learning and teaching. This Jewish law rule may still be applied by rabbinical courts, which determine "the welfare of the child" primarily from the religious point of view: the civil courts which determine "the welfare of the child" upon different considerations, regard that *halakhic* rule as obsolete. The Court did make an attempt to reconcile the secular (statutory) rule with the *halakhic* one, applying Jewish law for this purpose: We find that those who are by duty bound to learn, are by duty bound to teach, while those who are not bound to learn themselves, namely women, are not bound to teach (Kid. 29b). Meanwhile, however, girls are (by secular law) in duty bound to learn, and mothers like fathers are in duty bound to teach or educate; so that by applying the talmudic dictum of the interdependence of the duties to learn and to teach, the result is reached that the father, not having any duty of learning or teaching unshared by the mother, also has no corresponding right of custody beyond that of the mother. Custody rights having *halakhic*ally been tied to teaching duties, the principle - said hence to arise from Jewish law - was established that what is at stake in custody matters is not any right of the parent, but solely the rights and benefits of the child.

Fourth: A statute enacted for a Jewish religious purpose will be interpreted in conformity with *halakhah*. Thus, pieces of pork were held to be included in "pig" where the possession or sale thereof was prohibited, all the *halakhic* injunctions relating to pig extending also to pork (*Shulhan Arukh* Yoreh Deah 117).On the other hand, where a girl claimed to be exempt from army service - the statutory exemption being reserved for religiously observant girls only - the court did not enquire into minutiae of *halakhah* but held that the girl could not be expected to understand why army service should be prohibited to her: she was entitled to say, it is enough for me that the rabbis prohibit my serving in the army, and I regard myself bound by their injunctions even without understanding their reasons. But when a local authority made by-laws prohibiting the opening of places of entertainment on Friday nights, a municipal court held the by-laws to be invalid, legislation for religious purposes being within the competence of the Knesset only. The same apples to administrative rulings: the denial of licenses to import non-Kosher food was held unlawful; and the Prime Minister's discretion to close down television and broadcasting on Friday nights was quashed as ultra vires.

Fifth: While the recourse to Jewish law in all the foregoing cases is grounded on statute, in some way or other, there is a category of application of Jewish law which is a purely judicial innovation - and one daring enough to be deplored by many, including judges on the Supreme Court. Where a case fails to be decided according to justice or equity or public policy, Jewish law (*takanat hatzibur, tikun haolam, darkhei shalom*) has been invoked time and again. When, for instance, the question arose whether a contract was void as being contrary to public policy, the Court said that "for determining what would our public policy be and require, what would our *tikun* be, we look to our own moral and cultural values": in that case, an exemption from liability for loss of life of passengers reflects a disregard for the life of human beings incompatible with fundamental principles of Jewish law. It is true that exactly the same result could and would have been reached on general principles, without recourse to Jewish law: the invocation of Jewish law may just have been an act of reverence or national pride. Or, where a man contracted to transfer title to a house to a woman with a view to living there with her after his divorce from his wife, two of the three judges turned to Jewish law to determine whether such a contract was contrary to public policy: one held the contract void as tending to undermine the sanctity of the Jewish marriage tie, and the other held the contract valid, marriage in Jewish law being a contractual bond which could be dissolved at the will of the spouses, and there being ample authority in Jewish law to validate contracts in contemplation of divorce.

Especially in the area of contracts, the general policy of Jewish law is not necessarily identical with positive *halakhah*. Where a contract is deficient in form (lacking *kinyan*) and for that reason unenforceable, the unenforceablility may afford a legal excuse or license not to perform it - but God is said to defray himself from a man who breaks his promise, because an ethically principled man will not evade his obligations on formal grounds (*M.B.M.* 4:2). There can be no *takanat tzibur* and no *tikun olam* within the meaning of Jewish law (as distinguished from *halakhah*) in breaches of promises or undertakings.

Where the defendant had undertaken to sell to the plaintiff property expected to devolve on him on his father's death, he argued that that undertaking was contrary to public policy, mainly because it was invalid by *halakhah*. Indeed, the *halakhah* had been settled according to the view that one could not dispose of property which was not yet in one's possession (B. M. 16a et al.); but the fact that a contrary view had been propounded in the Talmud (and was later adopted in practice by some authorities) was held to indicate that there could be no policy considerations based on Jewish law not to hold the defendant to his contract (cf. *Tosafot* ad Ket. 91b) In effect, the Court adopted, qua Jewish law, the talmudic dissent which was not received into *halakhah*.

When the Court was asked to reopen a final judgement and change its terms so as to give redress to a defaulting party whom an illness had prevented to comply in time, all the judges found themselves in agreement that "justice" required the redress to be given - but all Israeli, English and American precedents precluded the reopening of the case. The Court held that this was a case of *ones* within the meaning of Jewish law, by which non-compliance with a final judgement by reason of force majeure could afford cause for re-opening: as a matter of general principle, Jewish courts were empowered to expropriate from the one and appropriate to the other where there was no other way to enable them to do justice to the parties before them (Ned. 27 a-b, Git. 36b, Yeb. 89b, Maimonides *Hil. San.* 24:6). Not that Israeli courts would ever usurp any such expropriatory powers, but we adopted the principle underlying it, that courts must have the powers which are required to enable them to do justice between the parties, even though they were not so empowered by explicit legislation.

I said in that case that "whenever we see fit, in order to do justice, to deviate from established precedent, I first ask myself whether the guidelines we seek cannot be found in Jewish law. It is not that we are bound by Israeli or English precedents so long as we have not found some precedent in Jewish law, nor that Jewish civil (or criminal) law has any binding force so as to oblige us to follow it; it is that the justice we are obliged and eager to do will perhaps prove more secure and better founded if we can relate it to our ancient legal traditions and to the wisdom of our righteous sages."

Apart from the "application" by the civil courts of Jewish law in the ways described, Jewish law is referred to very often by way of *obiter dictum*, whether for purposes of comparison or for purposes of distinction. The comparison of Jewish law with the applicable Israeli law is the custom of a few judges who are well

77

enough versed in and familiar with our ancient sources; and there is no area of the law in which such comparisons do not abound. And the distinction of Jewish law is intended, mostly by the same few judges, to show that its rules are not adaptable to present-day conditions, or that Jewish law has taken a course of evolution and development different from that which would fit our system (e.g. the whole law of evidence and procedure).

Jewish law is, of course, always "applied" by rabbinical courts, insofar as it has been settled as *halakhah*. But rabbinical jurisprudence excelled in conservativism, often even in fundamentalism, and contributed nothing to the modernization or liberalization of Jewish law. Moreover, although purporting to use modern Hebrew, that is a language which could be comprehended by modern lawyers (not to speak of litigants), rabbinical courts write their opinions in the language and style of the responses of old: like the responsors they use Aramaic expressions and quotations, technical terms and abbreviations that are unfamiliar and mysterious - in fact they write in a cryptology that is intelligible only to the initiated. Any detailed in-depth analysis of rabbinical jurisprudence in Israel would require extensive research which has so far not been undertaken. It may reasonably be apprehended that any such research would result in a demonstration of how unsuitable and anachronistic *halakhah* is for our present needs, and of how exactly it should not be applied.

4.

The indiscriminate application of *halakhah* (as distinguished from the principles of Jewish law) may well prove fatal to the survival of a Jewish democratic state and of Jewish solidarity. It is not so much its religious coloring or origin which makes it suspect, as rather the monopoly which the orthodox establishment claims both for its interpretation and for the universally valid determination of its applicability. In the realm of marriage and divorce, for instance, it is the (Orthodox) rabbinical courts which have the last word not only on what the *din torah* is, but also when and to what extent it is to be applied here and now. It is - and, I am afraid, will remain - quite irrelevant what other contemporary *halakhic* scholars who do not belong into their inner circle, may think or postulate within the *halakhic* framework to be legitimate and feasible.

Let me illustrate the mischievous effect of *halakhic* impositions by some recent Israeli experiences. The undisturbed rest of the dead, and the respect due to their graves and remains, is good and uncontested Jewish law. But *halakhah*, as interpreted by the Orthodox establishment, finds itself confronted by two arch-enemies: archaeology, on the one hand, and anatomy and pathology, on the other hand. The archaeological battle started with the violent interference by zealots with excavation works in Jerusalem and Tiberias: They asserted for sure that in the digging grounds there were ancient Jewish graveyards. No scientific purpose can justify any interruption of the tranquility of the dead (and while their interest and concern is, of course, limited to the Jewish dead only, the non-Jewish dead buried there must be suffered to benefit from their vigilance, too). One may, of course, accidentally encounter human remains also when laying building foundations (and then have, under the building laws, to give notice to the authorities) - but if building contractors are not generally so vehemently assaulted, it may be because archaeologists dig purposely and deliberately; deeper and deeper, one layer after the other, and the discovery and exposure of ancient burying-places is an integral part of their objective. That their rescue from oblivion and their reconstruction or preservation can even be said to do the dead honor rather than dishonor, is considered irrelevant. If anybody should have expected the spiritual leaders of *halakhic* Judaism to raise their voice in protest and save Jewish law from disrepute and vilification, he would have been sadly mistaken (not that the non-orthodox Israelis entertain any longer any such expectations). Instead, the orthodox establishment, to wit, the Chief Rabbinate and the orthodox political parties, insisted that in the future no archaeological research be carried out in grounds which the Rabbinate considers to contain human remains. It does credit to the Israeli legislature that this preposterous proposition has not become law.

While archaeology is prone to disturb the dead for the purpose only of enhancing knowledge, anatomy and pathology disturb the dead for the purpose of saving human lives. While archaeology can resurrect only past history, anatomy and pathology may sustain the life of future generations. It is good and uncontested Jewish law that the preservation of human life is paramount to all law (*pikuah nefesh*) - but the *halakhah* postulates a strict interpretation of "human life": There must be a certain life, a particular human being, to be saved in order that *pikuah nefesh* can be invoked. No cognizance is taken of potential or future human lives: they cannot as yet be "saved", because they are not as yet in existence. Medical use of dead bodies must, therefore, fall within the category of prohibited interference with the dead. This is another instance of a fundamental principle of Jewish law - the paramount sanctity of human life - being *halakhic*ally minimized so as to frustrate its application within its full potential.

Again, the orthodox protagonists of outright prohibition of anatomy and pathology did not prevail. The law is that a living person may donate his future dead body to science, and that failing such living donation all his or her next-of-kin may after his death do so in his stead. Some *halakhic* authority was unearthed by which a person enjoyed autonomy over his own corpse, which upon his death seemingly devolves on his natural heirs - but this kind of donation is heartily discouraged, so much so that the living donation may be made only on the prescribed form, and each of the next-of-kin is entitled to a right of veto by refusing to join in the others' consent. (In certain exceptional cases, post-mortem examinations may be ordered by a court.) The orthodox aversion from anatomous exercises is, of course, shared by very many people not at all *halakhi*cally motivated, for whom the integrity of the human body even after death is axiomatic.

As far as anatomy is concerned, the law works smoothly enough (it was recently reported in the press that some universities had more donations than they could handle). However, the law applies not only to medical research, but also to surgical treatment - and the problems of its application have taken on new dimensions with the increase in transplanting surgery. One should have thought that *halakhi*cally the surgery was more easily justifiable than the anatomy, because here there was a certain human life at stake to which *pikuah nefesh* was applicable, but most modern responsors go the easy way in the footsteps of their predecessors of pre-transplant times and hold both the consent to and the execution of transplanting surgery to be, at least, undesirable (Steinberg 170). All are agreed, and the law provides, that no organ may be transplanted from a dead body without prior formal consent of either the deceased during his lifetime or his or her next-of-kin after death: it appears (to the legislature, too) more desirable to let a human being perish than to make immediate good use of a vital organ which can no longer be of (except, perhaps, mystical) use to its departed owner.

Another example of the grave danger posed by *halakhic* rule is afforded by the ever recurring demand to have the Law of Return amended so as to ensure, once and for all, that conversions will not be recognized unless performed *kehalakhah*, that is, according to *halakhah* as understood and interpreted by the Chief Rabbinate. The emphasis, however, is not on *halakhah*, but on orthodox hegemony: *halakhah* is what the orthodox rabbinate declares it to be. As far as non-recognized or non-orthodox rabbis are concerned,

all *halakhah* is deemed inaccessible and unfathomable: they are no
more capable (and no better qualified) to act and officiate
kehalakhah than a non-Jewish clergyman. There can be no debate
on the merits of *halakhah*, what must be the prerequisites and
procedures for a valid conversion (or, for that matter, marriage or
divorce): the whole debate turns on the monopoly of orthodoxy.

Let us, for the sake of argument, assume that according to
halakhah a non-orthodox conversion is always, *ipso facto*, invalid.
Such a *halakhic* rule, if introduced into Israeli law, would play
havoc with Jewish coexistence and solidarity - both in the State of
Israel and in the Diaspora. Not that any such danger would deter
the orthodox: they hold, fiat *halakhah et pereat mundus*, let the
halakhah be fullfilled and the world perish, and their conscience is
laid at rest by denying the danger to exist (Yeb. 92a, San. 6b et al).
On the contrary, they say, the unity and uniformity of the Jewish
people is in jeopardy if non-orthodox conversions (or marriages or
divorces) were to be admitted. Their attitude appears to be
dictated by a preoccupation with orthodox Judaism rather than by
any regard for or cognizance of non-orthodox Jewry, and whenever
a question of survival arises, there can in their minds be no survival
of Judaism, or no value in such survival, unless it is orientated on
the orthodox version of *halakhah*.

This is also a good illustration of the misuse of the term
halakhah. As proposed to be used in the Law of Return, the term
does not mean Jewish positive law to be found in our ancient
sources, but norms of adjudication and qualification laid down from
time to time by the Israeli rabbinical establishment. It is not a legal
(or lego-religious) test, but an administrative (or politico-
religious)one; it has ceased to be religious law and has become
religious politics.

The search for *halakhah* as practicable Jewish law is,
therefore, rapidly assuming the character of pursuit of windmills.

The non-quixotic will search for meta-*halakhic* Jewish law for its own sake, and not indulge in illusions of practicability.

A no less deterrent example of a similar danger is provided by the public (and parliamentary) debate which has for a long time been, and still is, raging over our Bill of Rights. The orthodox parties strenuously oppose the enactment of a "Constitution" guaranteeing civil rights and liberties, on the pattern of modern human rights legislation: according to them, a gross violation of *halakhic* norms would ensue, nay the very Jewishness of the State would be jeopardized, if such like right and liberties were to be made constitutional bulwarks. Take freedom of movement: there can be no such freedom, they say, unless constitutionally restricted to the six weekdays. Or freedom of speech: there cannot be any such freedom, they say, unless blasphemy is constitutionally interdicted. Not to speak of the freedom of religion and religious worship which - insofar as Jews are concerned - is, of course, the exclusive preserve of the orthodox.

Ample authority can be found in Jewish law for each and all of these fundamental human rights, even such as they are understood today. The *halakhic* mind, however, is not at all concerned with any such purely *agadic* pronouncements. Nor does it matter to the orthodox that they bring Jewish law into disrepute or that their objections and obstacles deteriorate the standing and quality of Israeli law and legislation. Their sole purpose is to have *halakhic* norms, and eventually *halakhic* ways of life, imposed by the legislature to the largest possible extent. It is a rather small consolation that, in the nature of things, they succeed much better in preventing than in compelling legislation. And there is in the foreseeable future no reasonable prospect for a "Constitution" to be enacted by outvoting their objection; and if a "Constitution" is passed with their concurrence, I am afraid it will not be worth while enacting.

83

5.

To sum up:
(1) "Jewish law" is autonomous, comprehensive, non-coercive legal heritage of Israel. While *halakhah* is an integral part of Jewish law, it occupies - for the non-orthodox - no preferential position within it.

(2) A democratic legislature would be untrue to its functions and its mission, if it were to adopt a law only for the reason that it was Jewish. In order to be legislatable, a norm must be just and reasonable in itself and apt to achieve the legislative purpose at hand. It is true that in a democracy, the legislature cannot be constrained, or expected, to fulfill its trust and always enact only the just and reasonable: if a majority votes for it, it is the unjust or unreasonable which becomes law. Secular legislation to compel *halakhic* performance or ritual, is *prima facie* an unreasonable exercise of legislative power. The fact that the majority votes for it adds nothing to the reasonability of either *halakhah* or the secular law. Nor does it derogate from the justice or other intrinsic value of Jewish law (including *halakhah*) if the secular legislature fails or refuses to enact it.

(3) As for the application of Jewish law, other than compelling the performance of *halakhic* ritual, our premiss is that it is not just and reasonable *per se*, nor ought to be presumed (until the contrary is proved) to be just and reasonable: selections and choices from the body of law are not only legitimate but rather indispensable: they will produce the raw material to be molded and belabored before being put to practical use.

(4) Belief in the divinity of Jewish law (or any part thereof) implies not only a preconceived notion of its perfection, but also an intangibility by unauthorized agencies. The unbeliever's concept of Jewish law is fundamentally different from, and incompatible with,

the believer's concept thereof: there cannot be any consensus between them, either regarding the essence or regarding the application of Jewish law. Any partial mutual accommodation involves an intellectual and ideological sacrifice by either or both of them.

(5) It does not derogate from the Jewishness of moral and legal principles underlying norms and propositions of Jewish law, that they are by now universally recognized, nor that they may have originated in, or been adopted by, non-Jewish legal systems. On the contrary: universality is one of the prophetic goals of Jewish law. The truly Jewish vision is of a future in which our own concepts of justice and peace will be common to all mankind. As Maimonides once (in the context of *pikuah nefesh*) put it: The laws of the *torah* have not been give to bring vengeance or hardship into the world - they have been given to bless the world with compassion, loving-kindness, justice and peace (Shab. 2:3). This is exactly what, indeed, they ought to be made to do.

References:

G. F. Moore, *Judaism in First Centuries of the Christian Era* New York, 1971

B. Croce, *History of the Story of Liberty*   New York, 1955

M. Fishbane, "Freedom and Belonging", Sleeper and Mintz (eds.), *The New Jews*, New York, 1971, pp. 215-218

R. Ihering, *Geist des römischen Rechts*, 1968

J. Bentham, *The Principles of Morals and Legislation* London 1789

M. Elon, "The Sources and Nature of Jewish Law and its Application in the State of Israel", *Israel Law Review* Vols. 3 and 4, 1968, 1969

A. Steinberg, *Hilkhot Rofim Urefuah*, Jerusalem, 1978

* Much of the material here presented is taken from two papers previously published by me, namely: "The Methodology of Jewish Law - A Secularist View", Jackson (ed.), *Modern Research in Jewish Law*, Supplement One to the *Jewish Law Annual*, 1980 and "Jewish Law in Israel", in Jackson (ed.), *Jewish Law in Legal History and the Modern World*, Supplement Two to the *Jewish Law Annual*, 1980.

Pesikah and American Reform Responsa

The Early Years

Walter Jacob

The new Freehof Institute of Progressive *halakhah* will provide us with a forum for a better philosophical basis for the development of Liberal *halakhah*. Equally important is an analysis of what has been done thus far through responsa and various handbooks. Those efforts will continue to have a practical impact on Reform Jewish life and on our constituents in many lands. Even while we encourage philosophical and theological speculation we must similarly emphasize our practical efforts. There will be no *halakhah* without responsa. The very writing of the responsa indicates that we are continuing as a *halakhic* movement whether the philosophical basis is absolutely clear or not. This paper will review the early years of American Reform responsa.

Strange as it may sound to some the Reform movement virtually began with responsa. Just eight years after Israel Jacobson dedicated his Reform temple in Seesen,[1] and only a year after the establishment of the larger Temple in Hamburg,[2] a collection of Reform responsa entitled *Nogah Hatzedek* was published in Dessau (1818). The authors represented in this slim volume, Joseph Hayim, Ben Sasson, Jacob Recanati, Aaron Chorin and Eliezer Lieberman each defended the new movement in the traditional fashion. These responsa in Hebrew with their classic citations and traditional discursive style were not addressed to the new Liberal Jews who sought to establish the Reform movement but to their Orthodox opponents. They sought to convince the traditionalists that the new movement was tied to tradition and possessed standing in it. In keeping with the literary style of the early nineteenth century responsa literature these pieces are flowery, rhetorical and cited quotations that were helpful as well as other which were only minimally useful. Both the language of responsa and the style used were strange to the proponents of Reform who sought a simpler more direct approach which emphasized the older sources both biblical and rabbinic and decried the needless complications brought by the scholars of the previous centuries. The volume as expected elicited an Orthodox response as well as some Reform reaction, but little more. In fact, even some of the traditionalists chose other weapons for their response and decided to write in German on such matters as the organ controversy and changes in the liturgy.[3] In the next century and a half until Hitler put an end to Central European Reform Judaism, *halakhah* generally and responsa specifically were not used as a vehicle of Liberal Jewish expression. In part this was due to the more conservative character of Liberal Judaism on the continent. Its rabbi referred to the *Shulhan Arukh* and its commentaries when asked a question and if changes seemed in order like those in the liturgy, personal practices, etc., they were made and then defended as necessary in the various journals available to the exponents of Liberal Judaism. Among such periodicals were Geiger's *Zeitschrift,* and Frankel's *Monatsschrift,* in the nineteenth century, as well as various annuals and more popular weeklies and monthlies then and to the twentieth century. At times lengthy and involved discussions of historic sources were used while on other occasions the authors argued entirely on the grounds of modern philosophy and logic.

Perhaps another reason for the lack of liberal responsa in central Europe lay within the structure of the communities. All were recognized by the government, state supported and governed by a council which included all factions in the community. This meant that extremism was generally avoided; despite clashes, care was taken to prevent a major break. The Central European Jewish communities were overwhelmingly composed of Liberal Jews who comprised three-quarters of the Jewish population in the Western lands. We should also remember that by the middle of the nineteenth century there was little need to defend themselves against Orthodox opponents who now existed mainly outside

Germany, if they wished to witness the problems of living Orthodox practice they only had to cross a few kilometers into Eastern Europe and they would be clearly visible.

The reasons for lack of responsa then are (a) the conservatism of the central European Liberal Jewish communities; (b) the communal structure; (c) liberal dominance of these communities.

Precisely the opposite kind of conditions led to the rise of the responsa literature in North America. When the Responsa Committee was established under Kaufmann Kohler in 1907, Reform Judaism represented the best organized and most vigorous element of the American Jewish community. It, however, faced an ever increasing number of immigrants from Eastern Europe who became interested in Reform Judaism, and who had many questions about Reform practices and thought. Furthermore as the American Jewish community was isolated and young, it had no traditions and so the more extreme Reform position had taken a greater hold in the United States than in Europe. When the Executive Committee of the Central Conference of American Rabbis discussed the formation of a Responsa Committee some members expressed the need to help students graduating from the Hebrew Union College to defend their positions with reference to the traditional texts. The discussion followed an earlier debate about the purpose and format of a Minister's Hand Book in 1906,[4] and other ways of assisting younger colleagues. The discussion which established the Committee limited its work and provided that they "shall publish their answers in the Yearbook under the revision of the Executive Committee."[5] The members of the Executive Board did not wish the Committee to create a new *Shulhan Arukh*. It is difficult to understand why the Committee should not report directly to the Conference. This may have been part of an expressed desire to limit the work of the Committee or it may have reflected the feeling that responsa were individual opinions. They would not be binding, but

89

would provide considerable material from the tradition. The choice of Kaufmann Kohler as chairman did, however, provide the Committee with status. As President of the Hebrew Union College and Honorary President of the Central Conference of American Rabbis, no person of greater standing could have been appointed. Kohler was active in the Central Conference and served on six other committees. His appointment as chairman may also have reflected the controversial nature of this committee whose path remained undefined; his chairmanship removed it from politics. The appointment of Kaufmann Kohler provided a link between the college and its graduates in the day to day conduct of their rabbinate which could in theory have had a major influence on the American rabbinate though that was not destined to occur. The committee could and eventually did serve as a brake on extremism, as a bulwark for those who sought a more traditional position, and as a way of helping to bring uniformity into ritual practice. Those possibilities existed when the committee was established although they were not Kohler's concern.

The real development of the responsa literature in the American Reform movement did not occur until the period immediately following World War II. A number of factors influenced this course. The growing traditionalism of Reform Judaism which has been influenced in part on the nostalgia of the more recent and second generation Eastern European Jews, and in part on a recognition that the earlier path of Reform Judaism had been too radical. This produced a new interest in the tradition and its literature. A second factor was the appointment of Solomon B. Freehof, a congregational rabbi with a real interest in responsa, as chairman of the Responsa Committee. For the last four decades under the guidance of Solomon B. Freehof, myself, and now Gunther Plaut, the Responsa Committee has been led by congregational rabbis. These developments will be discussed in a subsequent paper.

When we look at the development of Reform Jewish responsa literature and its models of *pesikah* we are really investigating almost a century of Reform responsa in America as virtually nothing has been written in other lands.

Let us look at each of the American writers of responsa as they follow each other through the course of this century. We will begin with some early American Reform efforts which antedated the establishment of a Responsa Committee.

Two short pieces published in the collection *American Reform Responsa* represent early statements akin to responsa and served the same purpose. They are Schlessinger's "Cremation from a Jewish Standpoint" (1891), and Isaac Mayer Wise's "Circumcision for Adult Proselytes" (1893). The statement on cremation marshalled considerable evidence from the textual sources with primary emphasis on Biblical material. Only the last section brought citations from the Talmud, Maimonides, *Tur, Shulhan Arukh, Sefer Hahinukh Semag* and *Halakhot Gedolot.* The statement is long and discursive in nature. A resolution on this subject was passed by the Conference the following year so this was in the nature of a background paper rather than a responsum.

Isaac Mayer Wise in his discussion of "Circumcision for Adult Proselytes" summarized earlier papers. He made an effort to present the arguments for and against circumcision historically with citations from the standard rabbinic literature. However, a large part of the essay argued with earlier pieces on the subject. This paper also concluded with a resolution which dealt with the general matters concerning the reception of converts and did not limit itself to circumcision. Both papers came to liberal conclusions.

91

Kaufmann Kohler (1907-1921)

Kaufman Kohler (1843-1926) came to the United States in 1869 two years after he had completed his doctoral dissertation. He began his American career by combining an active congregational rabbinate with scholarship and intellectual leadership of the American Reform movement, which was demonstrated clearly through his composition of the text for the Pittsburgh Platform in 1885. He was president of the Hebrew Union College from 1903-1923, and became Honorary President of the Central Conference of American Rabbis in 1901 after the death of Isaac Mayer Wise. His principal interests were theological and historical studies of religion which covered all periods from ancient Mesopotamia to modern times. Responsa and *halakhah* stood at the periphery of his concerns.

As we look at the responsa produced by Kaufmann Kohler, as chairman, we find him often uniting with David Neumark and with Jacob Lauterbach; he permitted others of his committee, which fluctuated in size to write responsa. It generally consisted of professors from the Hebrew Union College with a few others. No report was offered to the Central Conference until 1911, and that was oral. The chairman in his report of 1914 mentioned submitting questions to other members of the committee, but indicated that due to the late arrival he had only consulted Professor Neumark.

By 1913 six responsa were collected for a report to the Central Conference. During those early years there were either no questions or they were simply answered by the professors of the Hebrew Union College without much formality as they would have answered the inquiries of any former student. Perhaps eventually the correspondence of one of those early Hebrew Union College graduates will turn up such a *halakhic* exchange. During the years 1913, 1914 and 1916, the Chairman Kaufmann Kohler complained about the paucity of questions and urged that members of the

92

Conference utilize the committee. In 1917 Kaufmann Kohler suggested that the entire function of the Committee be transferred to the faculty of Hebrew Union College which may indicate that they had been answering the questions anyhow. The suggestion was never seriously considered. The Committee from the beginning seemed to function with relatively few or perhaps no meetings, nor were the responsa which were to be published circulated to the committee as a complaint from David Phillipson in 1915 indicated. However, the involvement of various Hebrew Union College Professors would suggest that there may have been some informal discussion on the campus with David Phillipson who was also in Cincinnati, perhaps excluded for political reasons. However, despite Kohler's handling of responsa alone or letting one of his faculty members write them, he did not curb dissent and on a number of occasions other opinions were published, as for example, in 1914 and 1918. By 1914 James Heller already hoped for a collection of responsa for "ready use;" this was somewhat premature to say the least.

During Kohler's chairmanship thirty-one responsa which dealt with fourteen different subjects were written. Most of the responsa treated with the ritual questions: burial and mourning (8), *kaddish* and *yahrzeit* (4), marriage (3), circumcision (3), mixed marriage (2), and *bar and bat mitzvah*. Surprisingly enough there were also two responsa which dealt with *kashrut*; the subject was not treated by the committee again until the 1980's. We should note that five of the responsa dealt with Jewish Christian relations, either mixed marriage or funeral and cemetery arrangements. During this period Kohler wrote ten responsa alone, six with Neumark, five with Jacob Lauterbach, and one with Rappaport. He permitted Gotthard Deutsch to write six responsa, Julius Rappaport one, and Samuel Mendelsohn one. Kohler as chairman presided only loosely as the nature of the responsa suggest. He was content with short answers with minimal citations, but did not object to a

93

different style. His cooperation with others opened that path for the future.

We can see from this list of responsa that there was a need to deal with the parameters of Reform Judaism, both in its relationship to the tradition and to the non-Jewish world. Kaufmann Kohler understood the establishment of these boundaries as one of his tasks. This was made plain in one of the first responsa issued by the committee in 1913. It begins with the statement "I wish to touch upon a subject involving the very principle of Reform..." He continued by emphasizing an *evolutionary* rather than a *revolutionary* procedure as "we want to build up, not to destroy." Kohler then proceeded with a brief history of *bar mitzvah* which was the subject of this responsum, and of congregational reading of the *Torah* in general. This discussion moved rapidly to Confirmation and its effort to broaden Jewish education. He concluded by discouraging *bar mitzvah* in favor of confirmation especially as he saw that girls "remain attendants" at divine services and prove to be powerful influences for religion at home.[6] There was little attention to sources in this responsum. Yet, in the next responsum which dealt with the *kaddish*, sources were cited, *halakhic*, *aggadic* and modern, but not earlier responsa.

There was a responsum by David Neumark (1866-1924) professor of philosophy at the Hebrew Union College, in the same year on *bat mitzvah*. As a professor, Neumark concentrated on philosophy and Talmud; as a student he had received the Mendelsohn Prize for *halakhah* at the Hochschule in Berlin. Although Neumark presented a strong case for young women and their education, he saw no point in *bat mitzvah*, even in congregations where *bar mitzvah* continued; girls should simply be confirmed. Interestingly enough he added the statement that a boy's Hebrew instruction might be valuable as he could be admitted to the Hebrew Union College at the age of fourteen while "this possibility is practically out of the question in the case of a girl." Neumark wrote six other responsa with Kohler and both signed them.

If we look at these two responsa, which are representative of the early efforts, we find a good bit of rational argumentation, but little in the way of sources especially responsa. Neumark quoted no sources while Kohler provided Josephus, *Masekhet Soferim* and *Midrash Rabbah*. For Confirmation he cited a variety of nineteenth century German sources by Loew, Herxheimer, Geiger and Phillipson. These responsa were far removed from the pattern of tradition. This was also true of the third responsum issued in 1913, "Times When Weddings Should Not Take Place," which was signed by Kohler and Neumark together. In a brief statement they dealt with the *omer* period, the three weeks between the seventeenth of *Tamuz* and the ninth of *Av*, the Ten Days of Repentance and *hol hamoed.* There were brief citations from the Talmud, *Shulhan Arukh*, and nineteenth century Reform proceedings, an essay by Landsberg and a statement from the Augsburg synod. The conclusion, clearly and decisively permitted weddings during each of these periods. The two additional responsa of this *Yearbook* dealt with blowing of the *shofar* on the Sabbath and reading Torah portion in the vernacular. Both were also signed jointly by Kohler and Neumark and contained only minimal citations of standard rabbinic literature. The responsum on the Torah portion in the vernacular lacked all formal citations. I do not know which of the signatures actually wrote these responsum; my guess would be Neumark as Kohler was busy with administrative duties. A search in the archives might provide a definite answer to this question.

There was a responsum in 1918 on a "Rabbi Officiating at a Christian Scientist's Funeral" by Kohler which prohibited the burial through three rational arguments with no citations. Jacob Rappaport, a member of the committee, took an opposing stand with a responsum filled with rabbinic citations and used them to show that Kohler was not abiding by the spirit of Reform Judaism. Kohler subsequently (1919) wrote a single paragraph appeal to the members of the Conference that his decision be followed.

This brief exchange marks one of the few occasions in which different positions were publicly debated. Another occurred between Kohler and Deutsch (1918 and 1919) over *nolad mahul*. Kohler had provided a single line answer from the hospital bed; Deutsch objected and the next year Kohler responded with a brief well argued piece which he hoped "will be ratified by the members of the committee and endorsed by the Conference."[7] The possibility for such a path was established through their encounters.

In three responsa that dealt with "The Burial on Non-Jewish Wives in Jewish Cemeteries" (1914, 1916, 1919), Kaufmann Kohler provided no rabbinic references and simply stated his reason guided by the traditional sources and his own Reform point of view which was permissive despite some hesitation. The only references were a footnote which provided some basic Talmudic citations. One of these responsa was signed by Lauterbach as well. Deutsch in a much longer responsum (1919) filled with citations disagreed and left the matter to local authorities.

Gotthard Deutsch (1859-1921), Professor of History at the Hebrew Union College, who served as acting president of the college during an interim in the year 1903, wrote six responsa. As a historian his approach was anecdotal, and he felt that theoretical principles were less important than personalities and personal involvement. For him the forces of work in history remained very much the same throughout all periods or combination of physical and spiritual. Deutsch's historic concepts were not reflected in his responsa except in a fundamental historic view shared by all Reform writers of responsa. He provided a thorough review of the entire range of tradition with many sources, Biblical, Talmudic, rabbinic as well as modern. The argument in the responsum on "Divorce of an Insane Husband" was thorough and clearly summarized at the end of the responsum. More than sixty citations were listed in these few pages. Here we see a difference in methodology of Deutsch and Neumark-Kohler. Even when Kohler dealt with the subject of a "Rabbi Officiating at Mixed Marriages" (1919), a matter on which he felt quite strongly, he cited only Mielziner's *Jewish Law of Marriage and Divorce* and his own *Jewish Theology.*

The six responsa of Deutsch provided plentiful citations. He was obviously far more interested in tradition and its sources as was also evident from the two responsa which he wrote on *kashrut.* One of them dealt with a new material, pyrex.[8] This trend of Deutsch was already evident in his responsum on the "Sale of a Synagogue"(1919). These responsa of Deutsch provided citations from the traditional rabbinic literature, commentaries, earlier responsa alongside Reform Jewish material from the nineteenth century.

Interestingly enough the next chairman of the Responsa Committee, Lauterbach, who signed a number of pieces along with Kaufmann Kohler did not cite traditional sources while working with Kohler, and seemed simply to have signed the responsa alongside Kohler. In fact Lauterbach complained once in 1915 that Kaufmann Kohler did not cite tradition sufficiently.

The responsum "How Should a Loan in Foreign Currency Exchanged in another Country be Repaid?" (1920) was written by Samuel Mendelsohn. It was the only responsum of this period which dealt with economic matters. The arguments were based on the talmud, the codes and responsa. The pattern of the argumentation, the style and the conclusion were traditional; they followed closely the form employed in nineteenth and early twentieth century Orthodox responsa. It would be interesting to know how and why this question was directed to the committee.

Jacob Z. Lauterbach (1922-1933)

Jacob Z. Lauterbach (1873-1942) taught at the Hebrew Union College for thirty-one years as professor of talmud from 1911 to 1934. He combined traditional Galicean learning with the modern critical approach to the text. When he came to the United States in 1903 at the age of 30 he brought rabbinic ordination from the Orthodox Hildesheimer Seminar and a doctorate from the University of Berlin. He began by writing hundreds of articles for the *Jewish Encyclopedia* and *Otzar Yisrael*, a Hebrew Encyclopedia. Subsequently he edited and translated the *Mekhilta* in a fine critical edition and wrote on the history of Jewish customs and practices. Lauterbach's approach to all his studies combined a thorough review of the text and a close analysis of the material often laboriously assembled. This was followed by casting the tradition into a new and critical framework. His interest in customs and folklore became stronger with the passing years and was sometimes expressed in the form of responsa. As chairman of the Responsa Committee for a decade he moved the committee into a new direction. Kaufmann Kohler who retired in 1922 and became honorary chairman seems to have taken no further part in the work of the committee. Lauterbach had served on the committee from 1914 onward and so had some experience with it. Twenty-two responsa were written during the next decade including one by Samuel Cohon (Marriage with a Brother's Widow, 1925) and one in which Lauterbach endorsed the decision of Henry Berkowitz (Burial from the Temple with Reference to Suicide, 1923). During this period Lauterbach wrote the responsa himself and referred to the committee only six times in the signatures. The largest number of responsa continued to deal with burial (6), followed by (5) with the synagogue, (3) with marriage, (2) with the rabbinate, (2) with the Torah , and on all other subjects there was only a single responsum (*Shabbat, shofar,* the Jubilee, naming, birth control, and autopsy).

Three responsa were written by Lauterbach during his first year. The question on "Marriages Between New Year and the Day of Atonement" (1922) was answered in a short paragraph as was the inquiry about "The Removal of a Dead Body to Another Grave" (1922). In these responsa he followed the style of his predecessor and provided only the simplest rabbinic sources. Lauterbach changed his approach, however, as he turned to the question of the "Ordination of Women" (1922) which led him to a lengthy essay with many citations from the Talmud, Midrash, codes, as well as responsa. After providing the traditional conclusion along with the reasoning from the sources, he provided a negative conclusion on two grounds, (a) this would undermine the authority of the Reform rabbi and remove him from the "chain of tradition", and (b) *klal yisrael.* He brushed aside practical considerations such as the dearth of rabbis as that could be solved in other ways. He could not see women in a position other than mother and homemaker; he felt that these roles would interfere with the rabbinate, as women rabbis should be married just as male rabbis, and they would not readily find a mate who would place himself into a subordinate position. We can see then that in this instance the principle of equality of men and women, which was an early hallmark of Reform Judaism, was pushed aside by the principle of *klal yisrael,* the authority of the rabbi as well as a generous dose of personal prejudice. The latter undoubtedly was a major factor as more space was devoted to it than the other issues. Here Lauterbach in contrast to his other decisions was not liberal.

This was one of the very few responsa which was subjected to a lengthy debate by the Conference despite the original decision of the Conference to accept responsa as non-binding and without debate. Among those who spoke only David Neumark provided arguments with citations from the traditional literature in favor of the ordination of women. Lauterbach faced opposition from the general membership of the Conference as well as from his own committee. The committee members made no reference to any prior discussion of the responsum which seems to have been the work of Lauterbach alone.

Eventually a resolution of a special committee of the Central Conference of American Rabbis stated "we declare that women cannot justly be denied the privilege of ordination." This lukewarm endorsement kept the matter alive theoretically but did not lead to women entering the rabbinate for several decades until 1972. No vote was taken by the Conference and the Hebrew Union College decided against the ordination of women at that time.

Subsequent responsa of Lauterbach were often also brief; they dealt with practical questions like "The Position of the Synagogue Entrance and Art" (1927), "The Blowing of the *Shofar*" (1923), and "The Direction of Graves in the Cemetery" (1923), and were provided in a limited fashion with appropriate citations. He used other questions to write lengthy essays as for example, "Autopsy" (1925), "Birth Control" (1927), "Worshipping with Covered Heads" (1928), "The Naming of Children" (1932). In these essays as well as in some of the other medium length responsa, "Blowing of the *Shofar*" (1923). "Work on a New Synagogue on the Sabbath by Non-Jews" (1927), quotations from the Talmud and codes as well as responsa were generously used. In all of these responsa Lauterbach frequently provided an ingenious interpretation of traditional texts. Sometimes his responsa were misunderstood by readers, as for example the responsum which deals with "Worshipping with Covered Heads" (1928) was not intended as an endorsement for either covering or uncovering one's head but was written to demonstrate that this is a matter of custom not principle, and so should not be elevated to a position of extraordinary importance.

With the statements on autopsy and birth control the responsa committee moved into the area of medical ethics which was to occupy it often during the coming decades. The responsum on autopsy was thoroughly argued from a Liberal point of view. The issue of birth control was subjected to a more rigorous examination and Lauterbach demonstrated the restrictive nature of traditional Judaism during the last two centuries. It was a classical example of a full, thoroughly researched Reform responsum. In it he permitted the Tradition to unfold as he drew his own conclusions from the material. This was different from several other responsa in which he began with a definite Reform point of view and placed the material into that context.

We must ask why Lauterbach wrote at great length on some questions and only briefly on others. This seems to have been entirely due to personal interest. Those subjects which intrigued him led to long essays while others were disposed of with the simplest of statements. It would, for example, have been possible to write at great length on the status of non-Jews in the responsum "Work on New Synagogues on the Sabbath by non-Jews" (1927), after all, Jacob Katz was later to write a book on this subject, but Lauterbach chose not to follow that path. If he had been more interested in synagogue architecture the responsum "Position of Synagogue Entrance and Art" (1927) would have led him in that direction, but that was not his concern.

Two responsa written by others during his chairmanship followed very different paths. The responsum by Henry Berkowitz (1857-1924) "Burial from the Temple" with reference to "Suicides" (1923) was in the earlier tradition of Kaufmann Kohler. Berkowitz was a member of the first graduating class from the Hebrew Union College in 1883. He is chiefly remembered for founding the Jewish Chautauqua Society. It was written in the transition between Kohler and Lauterbach and it provided an answer with absolutely no citations from the Tradition. The answer was in keeping with the

101

traditional material, but that was never demonstrated. There was a responsum by Samuel Cohon's on "Marriage with a Brother's Widow (1925). Samuel Cohon (1888-1976) was professor of theology at the Hebrew Union College with a major interest in liturgy which he demonstrated through editing the *Union Haggadah* and being involved in the various additions of the *Union Prayerbook*. Cohon wrote in many fields including philosophy, rabbinics and theology. The responsum was thoroughly researched along traditional lines and presented material from the Bible, Talmud and codes as well as modern studies. Nothing from the responsa literature was cited and a great deal of the analysis dealt with modern critical studies.

This responsa was subjected to debate at the Conference; the Chairman of the committee, Jacob Lauterbach, disagreed with Cohon and his position that the rabbinic prohibition should be maintained. Cohon's position was accepted by the Conference.

Although Samuel Cohon published no further responsa he did write answers akin to responsa to inquiries by former students; I have seen some of them. They make references to the classical sources and codes with little or nothing from the later responsa literature. The questions with which he dealt were addressed to him by rabbis in a private fashion.

Jacob Lauterbach through his emphasis on rabbinics and Talmud moved the Responsa Committee in a new direction and gave it an impetus to review the rabbinic material in a scholarly manner. His efforts placed Reform responsa on an entirely different footing. It meant that Orthodox objections would have to be well grounded in the literature as these lengthy pieces could not simply be shrugged off. The number of responsa during this period remained small. Without doubt there were additional exchanges of letters between Lauterbach and his students and other members of the Central Conference on simple questions which he answered briefly in a personal way. To the best of my knowledge copies of those letters have not been preserved or collected.

Jacob Mann (1934-1939)

When Jacob Mann (1888-1940) became Chairman of the Responsa Committee in 1934, it was without any prior experience on the committee or for that matter much direct contact with the Central Conference of American Rabbis. Mann joined the faculty of the Hebrew Union College after receiving a doctorate in England as well as Orthodox *semikha*. During five of his six years as chairman, no reports were given to the Central Conference and in that single year (1936) only four responsa were written, always signed with the committee. When Jacob Mann again dealt with the question of the burial of a non Jewish wife with her husband in a Jewish cemetery, he rejected Kaufmann Kohler's earlier permissive stance. He did not discuss Kohler's responsum and seems to have felt no obligation to do so and always signed "Jacob Mann and the majority of the committee."

Jacob Mann's interest lay elsewhere and so he neglected his chairmanship. The committee hardly functioned during these years when major changes in the Reform Movement were taking place. Nothing of the debate surrounding the acceptance of the Columbus Platform is reflected in the work of the Responsa Committee.

The work of the first three chairmen of the Responsa Committee allows us to draw some preliminary conclusions about responsa in North America until 1940. The author has prepared another essay which discusses the later history of the committee. The Committee seems to have functioned primarily as a resource for Reform decisions. The need for this seems to have been felt more keenly by some leaders of the Conference than by its members, and so the number of actual questions remained small. There may have been an intent to use the Committee as a way of strengthening the influence of the Hebrew Union College Faculty within the Central Conference. That path may have been also indicated by the fact the first three chairmen were members of the Hebrew Union College faculty and that virtually all the responsa were written be the members of the faculty. However, this was not the road of the future.

The whole notion of issuing responsa through a committee represented an interesting American innovation yet this proved to be a mechanism rarely used. If we look at the committee under Kohler, we will see that the committee began with a full complement of eight members in 1908, but from 1909 to 1912 it consisted of only the chairman and Deutsch or the chairman and Neumark. From 1913 onward the composition varies from four to nine members. In that year Jacob Lauterbach joined the committee, in 1916 Jacob Rappaport and in 1922 Israel Bettan as well as Solomon B Freehof for a two year period. When there was a full committee it did not function as a committee, although there may have been some informal discussion.

The responsa themselves demonstrate a balance between Reform and Tradition. When no change in the Tradition was necessary, it was followed. During the chairmanship of Kohler and Lauterbach there was no effort to move toward Tradition. Even citations were few and the decisions were sometimes made without any traditional sources at all. The chairmen exercised only loose control over the committee and there seems to have been no formal meetings. We can point to no clear patterns for Kohler or Lauterbach's decisions; they were overwhelmingly permissive and liberal. Neither chairman was sufficiently interested in responsa to make them central or to write about *halakhic* theory. Both were willing to open this forum to others who wished to write for the committee; the style may have been different, but the spirit of the decisions remained the same.

The appointment of a third chairman, Jacob Mann, may have represented an effort on the part of the appointing president to limit the scope of the Responsa Committee or to remove it from the intense debates of the thirties. Intentionally or accidentally this certainly succeeded.

If we look at the committee in 1940 we find it moribund with an uncertain future. However, the nature of Reform Judaism had changed and the quiet half decade belied the more vigorous future which lay ahead. It wil be discussed in a subsequent essay.

1. July 17, 1810

2. December 11, 1817

3. Alexander Guttmann, *The Struggle of Over Reform in Rabbinic Literature*, p. 3 ff.

4. *Central Conference of American Rabbis Yearbook*, New York, 1906 pp. 61 ff.

5. *Central Conference of American Rabbis Yearbook*, New York, 1907 pp. 122

6. W. Jacob, (ed.) *American Reform Responsa*, New York, pp. 81

7. *Central Conference of American Rabbis Yearbook*, New York, 1919, pp. 75

8. W. Jacob, (ed.) *American Reform Responsa*, New York, pp. 131 ff.

Reform Responsa as Liberal *Halakhah*

W. Gunther Plaut

I

Reform Judaism began as a movement to reform *halakhah* and not, as its name might suggest, Judaism itself. Nothing was farther from the founders' minds. In fact, they did not even aim at remaking *halakhah* itself, rather, they aimed at reforming its thrust.

They accepted its process and premises. The process consisted of an orderly investigation of precedents, and the premise was, and remained, to discover how the Jewish people could live in accordance with God's will. But its thrust was changed, slowly at first and then with increasing rapidity and vigor. While the old method was to rely on the wisdom of earlier scholars who had already limned a solution to the issue in question, the new approach gave to contemporary scholars a far greater and more critical role. It did not assume that *halakhic* insight rested primarily on a corpus of past decisions. Rather, while it took earlier sages into respectful consideration it accorded modern scholars the right to assess the problem afresh and make informed decisions.

There was, of course, good reason both for this shift and for the resistance it engendered. The Emancipation had let fresh air into the dusty chambers of the ghetto, and with it came the unprecedented task of absorbing new conditions into the fabric of Jewish life. The new *halakhic* scholars were not afraid to accept valuable insights of modern non-Jewish culture, and especially its scientific methods. The old guard disagreed fundamentally with this. It continued to assert that Jewish tradition had all the answers and did not stand in need of outside knowledge. It considered all efforts to wed the world to the ghetto as a *pithon peh*, an opening to the forces of assimilation and apostasy. The liberals tried to retain the essentials of Judaism while accepting the opportunities of the Gentile world; the conservatives (as they were then called, the term orthodox was still in the future) decried every such attempt as hukqat *hagoi* and its purveyors as heretics.

This explains the extreme language of the traditional rabbinic responses which were issued as counterweights to the first *halakhic* tracts of the reformers, and it is sad to contemplate that 175 years later the tone has not changed. Whatever we Progressives say matters little; we are still the same heretics and apostatizing seducers. I have often wondered what might have happened if the principles of *talmud torah im derekh eretz* had been introduced at an earlier time and had not awaited the appearance of Samson Raphael Hirsch, when it was too late. But that, of course, is idle speculation; history is uni-directional. By the mid-nineteenth century the reformers had gone far beyond their original intent and both sides had already staked out inviolable territories.

By its very nature *halakhah* is a historical term. Strictly speaking it is the way of the past applied to our time, and so for that matter is Progressive Judaism itself. At its best, it is a movement "on the way" - which is to say that its thrust must be powered by an *halakhic* thrust. Progressive Judaism without *halakhah* quickly deteriorates into forms of ethicism and becomes a foil for convenience. *Only the strengthening of the halakhic impulse can keep our movement healthy,* and therefore an inquiry into the nature of a liberal *halakhah* becomes important, nay, imperative.

II

The earliest reforms, introduced in 1810 and thereafter in various German cities, were by today's standards quite modest. For reasons which are not clear even today, *Sefardi* pronunciation of the prayers was one of the innovations, as was the confirmation of girls, the introduction of the sermon in the vernacular, and the omission of a few *piyutim*. Only one theological change surfaced and that was the petition for *shivat tziyon* which was replaced by a more general prayer for *geulah*. As an aside, it is interesting to note that the *Sefardi* pronunciation and the German *derashah* became more contentious than all else; quite clearly, socio-political considerations were then already more important than either pragmatic or theological matters.

The conservatives decided on a path which had unsavory precedents: they invoked Gentile state authority to suppress the "heretics." The *Mitnagedim* had already done it in Lithuania to control the Hasidim; now the Prussian minister was importuned to close the Berlin temple. In 1817 the rabbis asked the Gentile state to intervene and stem further changes; in 1990 they ask the Jewish state to do the same. The approach is the same: it invokes the force of the state in order to stem religious reform. It was and is a short-term diversion; it did not succeed then and will not now. What was worse, it diverted both sides from engaging in meaningful dialogue over the nature of *halakhah* and the needs of the modern world. That was and is a pity, for today no less than in those days Jews all would benefit from such an interchange.

But to return to the early liberal *halakhah*. It must be admitted it produced no memorable lights, but at least it tried; the conservative opposition on the other hand did little more than use invective and chose not to engage in serious argument of an *halakhic* nature.

The opening thrust came with a collection put together by a certain Eliezer Liebermann, whose background seems somewhat murky. Still, he had the initiative to ask several rabbis of repute to issue *teshuvot* on various questions, and he published them in a small volume which he called *Nogah Hatzedek*.

One of the respondents was Rabbi Shem Tov Samun of Livorno who addressed himself to the permissibility of playing the organ in the synagogue. He defended it against the accusation of hukqat *hagoi* by saying that imitation of Gentile custom was forbidden only if imitation itself was its purpose; here however the reformers dealt with an ancient Levitical practice that had fallen into disuse. Rabbi Jacob Recanati of Verona agreed, but insisted that on the Sabbath the instrument be played by a Gentile.

The most interesting of these earliest Reform responsa was that of Rabbi Aaron Chorin of Arad in Hungary, who dealt with a variety of topics, among them the use of an organ, Sefardi pronunciation, and prayer in the vernacular. He argues in the accepted rabbinic fashion and did so with assurance. He was not yet speaking as part of a structured movement, but his presentation set the tone for many similar arguments to follow. Liebermann had asked him to respond to some of the questions that had arisen around the Hamburg Temple innovations and Chorin squarely came down on the side of the innovators. In effect he said: You want to know whether to do this and that it is permitted? My answer is yes, and here are the reasons and the sources to back up my judgement.

The effect of this small collection of Liebermann's separate tract *Or Nogah* on the Establishment was enormous, and they forthwith issued a counter-collection containing no fewer than 28 responsa. But, since these rabbis had little experience in a deviate that advocated unheard-of changes, their arguments with few exceptions were weak, *ad hominem* or simply dismissive. Thus, Rabbi Mordecai Benet of Nikolsburg wrote: "Be it far from us to accept any teaching from him [Chorin] concerning any kind of religious subject, for this man has only a mediocre knowledge of Talmud and commentary and usually occupies himself only with secular sciences."

And Rabbi Eliezer of Triesch in Moravia dismissed the whole treatise as a lie and said that in Hungary there were Jewish teachers whose students had greater knowledge than "this man from Arad."

The Hamburg innovators were dismissed by the Beth Din of Prague, headed by Rabbi Eleazer Fleckeles, as people who "really have no religion at all...Basically they are neither Christians nor Jews." The Hatam Sofer of Pressburg agreed and judged them to be persons who "really have no faith."[1] Not all that much has changed on the side of our detractors.

This is the period which, in another context, I have described as one in which the reformers approached every inquiry with another question: *Mah yomru haavot?* What does tradition have to say on this issue? The questions and responses were cast into the traditional mode of *sheelot uteshuvot.* There was, however, an important difference: these new *teshuvot* were not generally asked in order to find out *ab initio* whether a particular departure might be permissible; rather, the departure had usually already taken place and the respondents tried to find a *halakhic* precedent that might legitimize it. The early reformers were therefore largely justifiers *ex post facto*; they wanted to issue a *heter* and found reasons for doing so. They did not come to questions of innovation with an open mind.

This is especially clear when we examine the proceedings of the first rabbinical conferences in Brunswick, Frankfort, and Breslau (1844-1846). In Brunswick a number of study commissions were formed; of which one was headed by Rabbi Joseph Maier of Stuttgart, who chaired the first convention and was later to head the Leipzig Synod. Maier's committee was to study reasons for the diminished appeal of religious services and bring back a report to the second conference in Frankfort, detailing proposals for a new liturgy.[2]

111

As was to be expected, the report strongly advocated liturgical reform which was to be marked especially by the introduction of prayers in the vernacular and other liturgical alterations. Having reached this conclusion Maier's report proceeded to present a historical Jewish prayer and did not hesitate on occasion to take issue even with the redoubtable Leopold Zunz. The age and origin of particular prayers was examined, as was the role of the cantor; the repetition of the *misheberakh* for each *aliyah*, added selections for the *haftarot*, and so on. Clearly the innovation -- or its need -- came first and the justification later, and this is attested by the occasional remark that a particular practice has already been introduced here and there.

There was, however, one report which followed the classical *teshuvot* more closely both in approach and content. It had to do with the permissibility of certain procedures which would make the installation of *mikvaot* in private homes feasible. The report was replete with scholarly material, but in the end it too showed its pragmatic purpose. It called on the convention to ease current rules for *mikveh* construction and hoped thereby to increase the observance of *taharat hamishpahah*.[3]

III

In the nearly 150 years which have passed since then, Progressive Judaism has gone through a number of cycles. In America especially *halakhah* fell more and more into desuetude, until even the word mitzvah disappeared from its vocabulary. Only a few *halakhic* restrictions could be said to be common to all Progressive Jews, which is to say that the authority of Tradition was replaced by the autonomy of the individual. Only from time to time did a few hints of connection with the old *halakhah* surface, and a few learned essays, such as those of Kaufmann Kohler on "The Four Ells of the *Halakhah*," and Jacob Z. Lauterbach on birth control and on covering the head, kept alive a nominal awareness of our *halakhic* past.[4]

To Rabbi Solomon B. Freehof belongs the distinction of having recreated a connection between this past and its Reform presence. First in his two books on *Reform Jewish Practice*[5] and then in eight volumes of collected Reform responsa he guided the leaders of the Progressive movement toward asking questions about such connectivity. Tradition, he said, had a voice but not a veto, and he did not wish his work to be considered a new *Shulhan Arukh*. In his responsa he detailed with great scholarship how traditional decisors approached the question under consideration and on occasion he speculated how they might treat it today. But at that point he stopped. He took their advice on most occasions because he saw no particular reason not to take it; but when he did depart from it he rarely gave reasons that were grounded in any Progressive thought system. Then he would simply say, in effect, "We do not do it that way." The past was instructive, but not decisive, and Reform *minhag* was given pragmatic preference when the chips were down.

Still, the overwhelming weight of Freehof's conclusions is based solidly on Tradition. To take but one example, he was called upon to decide the *kashrut* on a *mezuzah* that was rolled in such a way that its text was legible to the outside. Freehof called this "absolutely wrong," but did not say why -- in a Reform context -- this should be so when other departures from Tradition are permitted.[6]

Because he had not specified when traditional *halakhic* practice might be put aside Freehof, was faced with a dilemma. If, as he and the Progressive movement have always stressed, we represent an authentic development of Judaism and stand in the tradition of our faith and people, then our way of developing Judaism is as valid as any other way. But at the same time we are

113

also aware that we have departed from *halakhah* as it has been known over the centuries, and our *teshuvot* are not just ordinary responsa, they are of a different brand. Do we therefore belong in a volume of Jewish responsa literature or do we not?

Freehof's basic approach would lead us to expect that we most certainly do belong, yet in his own exposition of such literature, *A Treasury of Responsa*, he excludes us. Thus, he finds no place in such a compendium for the model *teshuvot* by Lauterbach, but he does include a responsum by the Lubavitcher rebbe.[7] The contradiction is palpable.

Freehof's successor in the chairmanship of the Central Conference of American Rabbis Responsa Committee, our colleague Walter Jacob, has carried on his mentor's scholarship with great distinction, and the volume he has published of his own responsa is a splendid addition to our literature.[8] His decisions are cast in the Freehofian model, and no attempt is made to give his conclusions a comprehensive historical or theological basis.

Some years ago, when I contributed an essay to Bernard Martin's collection *Contemporary Jewish Thought*,[9] I tried to deal with this problem and came to the conclusion that the very use of the word *halakhah* for both traditional and Reform responsa was a source of confusion. Because we viewed the *halakhic* system from a different perspective I proposed to make the distinction more evident by using a similar yet different term, and proposed that we should henceforth call our responsa literature *halikhah*, an old word that in legal respects carried no ballast. My suggestion stayed where it was put: between the pages of small volume with limited circulation, and I am not about to revive it.

However, I am convinced that the time has come to make up our minds how we can unambiguously resolve the dualism of our approach, that is to say, how we can stand both in the authentic tradition of the Jewish people and at the same time present a new interpretation.

I propose a somewhat different approach, and in my brief incumbency as chairman of the Central Conference of American Rabbis Responsa Committee I have tried to apply it to the few decisions we have made so far.

I proceed from the recognition that we now have some 170 years of Progressive tradition behind us. In the course of that span we have amassed a significant body of thought, have arrived at certain stated principles and have included them in resolutions and responsa. We are therefore now ready to state that our Reform responsa will be based on two considerations: on Tradition as well as on the legal corpus of our Liberal movement.

We begin with Tradition and ask: how does it treat this *sheelah*? We then proceed to ask: What is there in our Liberal tradition that would have us disagree? Is there a previous ruling or other legal document that would have us decide otherwise? If not, Tradition stands; if there is, we must examine how our Liberal *halakhah*, as developed so far, can be applied in the case before us. To take an obvious example, if we were confronted with a case in which the religious equality of women were at issue, our Liberal principles would be given decisive weight. But when we do this, it is imperative that we state and detail why we depart from Tradition, what principles and precedents guide us.

In this way we are in fact creating a new body of reference, a distinctly Liberal *halakhah* and we must have no hesitation to call it just that. We have no prospect of being accepted by the traditionalists, at least not now; but we may well set a pattern that will, in time, be seriously considered by those not of our movement.

But I must issue a warning: It is not enough to call, in a sentimental mood, on "Liberal principles." We are in the business of creating a distinct form of *halakhah*, and we must go by proper precedent - be it of the Traditional or the Reform type. Our decisions are not sermons, they are cast in a legal framework. And if all goes well and we continue on the path so well hewn out by our predecessors, our own people may come more and more to know that we exist and that they should carefully consider our decisions.

That is why the work of this new international Liberal effort to draw the various strands of our thought together and cast them into one systematic whole is so important. I regret that I cannot be present to celebrate its inaugural, but I do pledge my continued support to the valiant effort of our colleagues, Moshe Zemer and Walter Jacob. May they succeed, and we with them.

1. Details in W. Gunther Plaut, *The Rise of Reform Judaism*, New York, 1963, pp. 32 ff.; Michael A. Meyer, *Response to Modernity*, New York and Oxford, 1988, pp. 50 ff.

2. The report is reprinted in *Protokolle und Aktenstucke der zweiten Rabbiner-Versammlung*, Frankfurt am Main, 1845, pp. 285 ff.

3. *Ibid*, pp. 359 ff.

4. K. Kohler, *Hebrew Union College Annual* I
(1924), pp. 8 ff.; Lauterbach, *CCAR Yearbook* xxxvii (1927), pp. 369 ff.; *Ibid.* xxxviii (1928), pp. 589 ff.

5. Hebrew Union College Press, 1944 and 1952.

6. *New Reform Responsa*, New York 1980, p. 54.

7. *A Treasury of Responsa*, Philadelphia: JPS, 1963.

8. *Contemporary Reform Responsa*, New York, 1987.

9. "The Halakhah of Reform", Chicago, 1968, pp. 88 ff.

Between Antinomianism and Conservatism
The Need to Evolve an Alternative *Halakhah*

John D. Rayner

In the beginning God created the world in order that it should in time bring forth a species of autonomous creatures freely doing His will. To this end He created all human beings "in His image", that is, with a capacity to discern between right and wrong; He chose one people to spearhead the process of the fulfillment of His purpose, and entered into a Covenant with them; and He sent them messages concerning His will. Eventually these messages became the subject of a book, and the book was canonized. That is to say, the priestly leaders taught the people to believe that it contained the actual divine messages rather than merely their ancestors' human interpretations and misinterpretations of them.

When religious leadership passed to the Pharisees, they reaffirmed that myth, and added to it another: that of an equally ancient and sacred oral tradition, explaining, elaborating and supplementing the written text, and under the slogan *torah min ha-shamayim* made this two-fold myth the foundation of post-Biblical Judaism.

On that foundation the Rabbis, who succeeded the Pharisees, built a superstructure of legislation phenomenal in its comprehensiveness, for it covered every aspect of life, and in its specificity, for it considered no detail too minute to merit attention.

This stupendous jurisprudential enterprise was not, indeed, the Rabbis' only activity. They also interpreted Scripture for edification; but the legal activity is what they took most seriously. To distinguish the two, they called one *agadah* (*hagadah* in Babylonia), from the expression *maggid hakatuv*, and the other *halakhah*, the Hebrew form of the Aramaic word *hilkheta* which is regularly used in the *targum* to translate such words as *mishpat* and simply means "law".

***

The rabbinic *halakhah* regulated Jewish personal, domestic and communal life for two thousand years until the Emancipation. Then, for most Jews, it lost its former authority: partly because rabbinic courts no longer had the power to enforce it; partly because social pressure, having previously worked in favor of conformity to Jewish tradition, now favored conformity to the lifestyle of the non-Jewish environment; but most fundamentally because the very basis of Rabbinic Judaism, namely the myth of *torah min hashamayim*, ceased to carry conviction.

The credibility of the myth, previously strained, now snapped because of the doubt cast on it by Bible criticism and, more generally, because the whole mentality which had preserved Jewish as well as Christian and Muslim scholasticism through the Middle Ages receded before the advance of the modern critical spirit. It was that which knocked the bottom out of Rabbinic Judaism.

Not, indeed, for all Jews. There were those, now called Orthodox, who barricaded themselves inwardly and outwardly against the encroachments of modernity. But they soon became a minority, and it was with the aim of keeping the majority within the Jewish fold that the Reform Movement came into being.

***

As with all such movements, the Reformers not only made changes but sought to justify them; and to this end, paradoxically, they often invoked the very tradition whose authority was now in question. But after some time that exercise was largely abandoned, both because its self-contradictory nature came to be perceived and because it became evident that no searching of the rabbinic *halakhah* for permissiveness could possibly justify the more far-reaching reforms now deemed necessary, such as the rejection in principle of priesthood and sacrifice, of *halitzah* or *halitzah* and *mamzerut*, and the granting of equal rights to women.

Halakhah was left to the Orthodox rabbinate, to whose jurisdiction one might have to make all sorts of concessions in practice, especially if one lived in a *Consistoire* or *Einheitsgemeinde*, but it was no longer a major concern of the Reformers. Progressive Judaism, especially in the English-speaking world, became antinomian. *Halakhah*, and related words like *mitzvah*, ceased to feature in its vocabulary. Instead, its expounders saw Judaism as consisting of two aspects: "beliefs" and "practices".

The "beliefs" were drawn mainly from the Bible, especially from Prophets, embellished with apt quotations from the Rabbis. They included something called the Moral Law, which was, however, a philosophical, not a legal, concept. They also included social ideals, which inspired men like David Einhorn to speak out courageously against slavery, and prompted the Central Conference of American Rabbis to embark on an ambitious programme of "social action", impressively recorded by Albert Vorspan and Eugene Lipman in their volume *Justice and Judaism*. But such social action was seen as an expression of Prophetic idealism rather than of Rabbinic *halakhah*. As Eugene Lipman confesses in his contribution to the little volume, *Liberal Judaism and Halakhah*, edited by Walter Jacob and published in Pittsburgh in 1988, "It is...a source of pain to me that we have not used rabbinic sources...in our social justice pronouncements."[1]

The "practices" of Judaism were identified with "ceremonies" or "rituals" or "observances", that is to say, the celebration of

121

Sabbaths, Festivals and lifetime events in synagogue and home. Compared with the "beliefs", they were considered of minor importance but nevertheless necessary, since every religion needs to have such "frills". They, too, therefore, were not thought of as part of a *halakhic* system.

***

The modern revival of interest in *halakhah* within Progressive Judaism owes much to the writings of Jakob Z. Lauterbach and more to those of his disciple Solomon Freehof, whose two-volume work, *Reform Jewish Practice and its Rabbinic Background*, written during the Second World War, may perhaps be regarded as the watershed. But it was after the War that the shock of the Holocaust and the establishment of the State of Israel combined to bring about an intensified concern for Jewish unity and continuity and, with it, an enhanced appreciation of the significance of *halakhah*.

Since that time there has been, for instance, a huge increase in the publication of Responsa by the Central Conference of American Rabbis Responsa Committee and especially by its late Chairman Solomon Freehof as well as his successor Walter Jacob, who, in his contribution to *Liberal Judaism and Halakhah*, informs us that he received over 100 questions a year![2] There has manifested itself in many of our movements, notably the RSGB, a new willingness to consider and to reinstate traditional *halakhic* procedures in such matters as conversion. And Moshe Zemer's numerous articles in the Israeli press have done much to show that the *halakhah* can be effectively invoked, not only to justify the policies of Progressive Judaism but also to give ethical guidance on burning social and political issues.

It must be said that there has also been a reaction against this renewed emphasis on *halakhah*, of which more anon, and there is certainly a wide range of opinions among us as to what our relationship with the *halakhah* should be. In addition, there is in some quarters a strongly felt concern about the existing divergences of practice between different constituents of the World Union, as highlighted in particular by the patrilineality debate.

Not surprisingly, these issues have tended to dominate the debate whenever international gatherings of Progressive rabbis have taken place, usually in conjunction with World Union conferences. It was at one of these, in Jerusalem in 1976, that the view was first expressed that it might be helpful to set up an international agency for mutual consultation and co-operation in this area, and at the 1980 conference, also in Jerusalem, I elaborated that suggestion in a paper entitled "Towards a World Union *Halakhah* Committee". There then followed a protracted attempt to establish such a committee, which, however, for reasons best left unexplored, came to nothing. All the more gratifying is it to me, and I hope to all of us, that, thanks to the initiative of Moshe Zemer and others, the project is now, after all, getting off the ground.

***

But if it is to succeed, then it is essential that those engaged in it should be very clear, and as far as possible in agreement, about what they are doing; and therefore we need to re-examine the diversity of attitudes to *halakhah* which exist in our movement.

At one extreme is the antinomianism to which I have already referred and which, though less typical of our movement than it used to be, still persists, perhaps more commonly among our lay people than our rabbis. But there is also a history of rabbinic antinomianism which stretches from Samuel Holdheim to Alvin Reines and his disciples.

Briefly summarized, the argument takes one or both of two forms. First, the *halakhah* has no authority for Progressive Judaism, which indeed recognizes no external authority of any kind, since its greatest virtue and chief if not sole defining characteristic is its radical acceptance of individual autonomy. Secondly, the paramount need of the, *nevukhei hazzeman*, the perplexed of our time, is to rediscover God, which is a matter of theology, or of spirituality, not of *halakhah*, which is therefore irrelevant as well as inappropriate.

The argument may sound plausible, but its implications, if they were taken seriously, would be disastrous. For to reject *halakhah* would be to reject one of the greatest elements of our Jewish heritage. It is *halakhah* which has kept us mindful of the need to translate the theory of our faith into practice, and to apply it to all aspects of life. It is *halakhah* (though not only *halakhah*) which has preserved the unity of our people through a tempestuous history. And it is *halakhah* which has elicited the most strenuous mental exertions of our scholars for two thousand years. In the words of Solomon Freehof, "The real intellectuality of our people, their real brilliance, their full sounding of the depths of human ability to think and to reason is in the *halakhah*. It is not an exaggeration to say that never in the story of mankind's intellectual effort has so large a proportion of one people produced so brilliant a succession of intellectual works."[3]

To reject the *halakhah* would therefore be an act of unthinkable self-impoverishment and self-emasculation. Which being the case we must go back to the antinomian argument and question its premises. Although the *halakhah* does not have a decisive authority for us, may it not have an advisory authority as a source of wisdom? Although the individual is indeed autonomous, does he not need guidance - from that source among others - so that he may exercise his autonomy responsibly? Does not a community, however liberal, need to have rules? And might

124

not the very exercise of trying to puzzle out the Divine Will, with respectful though not uncritical regard for tradition, be for many of the *nevukhim* a means of finding their way back to God?

***

But let us leave antinomianism there and turn to the opposite extreme. Strictly speaking, that is, of course, fundamentalism, which demands total subservience to a tradition conceived as having divine and, therefore, not-to-be-questioned authority. But since fundamentalism, in that sense, hardly exists in our movement, I would like to speak instead of conservativism, by which I mean those traditionalist and neo-traditionalist tendencies in Progressive Judaism which resemble the historic stance - though that may now be changing - of Conservative Judaism.

More specifically, I mean an attitude which rejects fundamentalism, but in muted tones; which hedges and wriggles rather than says out loud that this or the other biblical commandment is not divine; which speaks of the *halakhah* as if it were authoritative, without need to question the assumptions on which a particular law rests or to investigate the historical circumstances which gave rise to it; which claims that the *halakhah*, properly understood and imaginatively interpreted, contains all the flexibility necessary to make it serve contemporary needs, and on that basis claims to be in continuity with it.

I find that approach deeply unsatisfactory. First, because it fudges the issue of the authority of Scripture, which needs to be squarely faced. It sounds pious to speak of Scripture as sacred; but there are many biblical laws which seem to me so manifestly human and mistaken, that to hold God in any way responsible for them, far from being pious, is a *hilul hashem*. In this matter Louis Jacobs has often been more forthright than the neo-traditionalists in our camp. In his 1984 book *A Tree of Life*, for instance, he wrote

125

with commendable candor: "It can no longer be denied that there is a human element in the Bible" and that "it contains error as well as eternal truth." [4]

Secondly, the attitude I am discussing grossly overestimates the adaptability of the rabbinic *halakhah*. Of course it contains "diversity, flexibility and creativity" (to quote the sub-title of *A Tree of Life*), and a great deal more than is generally realized, as Louis Jacobs demonstrates in that book. But the room for manoeuvre within the traditional *halakhic* system is nevertheless limited, and nowhere near adequate for present needs. Solomon Freehof was surely right when he wrote: "There is no possible stretching of the law or liberalizing of it that can enable it to roof over the realities of modern Jewish life."[5]

Moreover, even if it were possible, it would be inconsistent with our integrity as Progressive Jews, because it would mean pretending that the *halakhah* was authoritative for us in a way which it plainly is not. For all its sometimes surprising capacity for change, the Rabbinic *halakhah* is fairly and squarely based on the myth of *torah min hashamayim*. To quote Louis Jacobs again, "None of the traditional *halakhists* ever dared...to take issue with, for them, the basic doctrine upon which the *halakhic* structure is reared, namely, the infallibility of Scripture in its rabbinic interpretation and the infallibility of the Talmudic rabbis as the sole and final arbiters of the *halakhah*."[6]

In many respects the premises of the Rabbinic *halakhah* are not our premises; their methods are not our methods; and the affirmations derived from those premises and by those methods are not our affirmations. Considering that whole vast areas of its contents relate to sacrifices and priesthood and ritual purity and male superiority and polygamy and *yibum* and *halitzah* and *mamzerut* and corporal punishment and capital punishment (which list alone accounts for about half of the *taryag mitzvot*), for

126

Progressive Jews to affirm such a system, subject only to a few cosmetic changes, is so bizarre that I can only understand it as either self-deception for the sake of the emotional comfort, or else propaganda for the sake of the political advantage, to be gained from a traditionalist posture. Indeed, it seems to me that in the rhetoric of the neo-conservatives in our Movement, the word *halakhah* is merely a synonym for "tradition", and doesn't noticeably go with any serious interest in *halakhic* literature, or have any point of resemblance with the kind of strenuous intellectual struggle to ascertain the Divine Will which I take the *halakhic* process to be.

Walter Jacob put it rather kindly when he wrote that "no consistent philosophy of Conservative *halakhah* has yet emerged."[7] I would say: it hasn't emerged because it can't emerge. To my mind the whole position is intellectually untenable. Furthermore, if I read the signs correctly, it is on its way out. At the 1980 Convention of the Rabbinical Assembly, Harold Kushner made the perceptive remark that "the Conservative movement has owed itself a crisis on the issue of the authority of *halakhah* virtually since its foundation."[8] What has brought the crisis to a head is the issue of women's rights. But there are other signs. For instance, the case for treating the children of mixed marriages alike, irrespective of whether the mother or the father is the Jewish parent, is so overwhelming that it has been adopted by the Reconstructionists and advocated by individual rabbis in the Conservative movement, and it can only be a matter of time before it becomes general policy throughout the non-Orthodox world.

***

If then both antinomianism and conservatism are to be rejected, we need to adopt an intermediate position. There are two main options. One of them avoids the use of the word *halakhah* altogether but nevertheless advocates a return to tradition; and if I say that it tends to employ the language of "Covenant" and

127

"*mitzvah*", you will understand that I am alluding to the philosophies, in their different ways, of Buber, Rosenzweig, Heschel, Fackenheim, Plaut and Borowitz.

I have a great deal of sympathy with that approach, but with two reservations. The first is that the word *mitzvah* tends to refer to acts of ritual, which, though not as unimportant as the Classical Reformers thought, are nevertheless less important than moral obligations. Indeed, they do not even raise questions of right and wrong, and hence of God's will; for though there is a "right" and a "wrong" way, for instance, to light the Shabbat candles, it is quite obvious that in such a context "right" and "wrong" do not have ethical connotations.

My other reservation is simply that I see no good reason why we should deprive ourselves of the word *halakhah*. There have been other kinds of *halakhah* in the past besides the Pharisaic-Rabbinic one. The Karaites, for instance, had their own *halakhah*; and there already exists a distinctive, Progressive *halakhah*, contained in hundreds of statements, resolutions, articles, responsa and, not least, prayerbooks.

And therefore the other option, which I have advocated in a number of lectures over the last twenty years[9], is that we should come out into the open and say that we wish to continue to do, but to do more systematically, what in effect we have been doing since the 19th century, namely to evolve an alternative Progressive *halakhah*, consonant with our task as pioneers of a post-rabbinic, post-medieval Judaism. For the question, *mah adonai eloheikha shoel meimakh* (Deut. 10:12), is the most important of all questions, for us no less than for former generations. It is true that for us there are no *certain* answers. But that does not mean that there are *no* answers. For we have four resources: Scripture, Tradition, Knowledge and Conscience. Not one of them is infallible, but all of

128

them have a contribution to make to the process of trying to puzzle out as best as we can what God requires of us in our time.

Our conclusions, therefore, will always be tentative. We shall present them, I hope, with due modesty, together with the thought-processes that have gone into them as well as any dissentient views that have been expressed, and we shall make it very clear that everything is subject to revision. We shall address ourselves, in time, to global issues, such as ecology; to political issues, such as peace; to social issues, such as business ethics, medical ethics and sex ethics; to communal issues, such as marriage and conversion; to congregational worship and to personal observance.

We need to wrestle with these problems, first as Jews concerned to know and do God's will; secondly as rabbis, called upon to give guidance to individuals and to help formulate the policies of our communities; and thirdly as citizens, so that, by the exercise of our democratic power to influence public policy, we may make a Jewish contribution to *tikun olam*.

1. Walter Jacob, ed. *Liberal Judaism and Halakhah*, Pittsburgh, 1988, p. 133

2. *Ibid.*, 93

3. Solomon B. Freehof, *Reform Judaism and the Legal Tradition*, London, 1961, p. 9

4. Louis Jacobs, *A Tree of Life*, Oxford, 1984, p. 242

5. Solomon B. Freehof, *Reform Responsa*, Cincinnati, 1960, p.13

6. Louis Jacobs, *A Tree of Life*, Oxford, 1984, p. 237

7. Walter Jacob, ed. *Liberal Judaism and Halakhah*, Pittsburgh, 1988, p. 100

8. Convention of the Rabbinical Assembly, *Proceedings*, 1980, p. 364

9. "Towards a Modern Halakhah" (Council of Reform and Liberal Rabbis, 10th February, 1970; published in *Reform Judaism*, ed. Dow Marmur, RSGB, 1973); "Rethinking our Attitude towards the *Halakhah*" (Conference of European Progressive Rabbis, Amsterdam, 29th June, 1970); "Towards a World Union *Halakhah* Committee" (Rabbinic Kallah, World Union for Progressive Judaism, Jerusalem, 27th February, 1980); "Developing a Progressive Jewish *Halakhah*" (Leo Baeck College, Summer Study Week, 24th June, 1985).

Halakhah and Sex Ethics

Hyam Maccoby

*H*alakhah is too often presented as a monolithic structure, in which all laws are of equal weight and all have similar Divine sanction. The reality is that the history of the *halakhah* is one of argument and differences of opinion, so that any decision, even when "fixed", is of a provisional kind, since it is the outcome of discussion and debate. Moreover, the provisional character of *halakhah* is itself sanctioned by Jewish tradition, which insists on preserving the dissident opinions as a basis for possible future contrary decisions (*Mishnah*, Eduyot, 1:5, and Maimonides' comments in *Mishneh Torah*, Mamrim, 2:1-2).

Further, a great source of flexibility in traditional *halakhah* is the preservation of distinctions between various types of laws in respect to their gravity. The greatest distinction is between laws that are *deoraita* (scriptural) and laws that are *derabanan* (rabbinical), but there are also important distinctions even within these categories. The result is a graded system of laws, so that, in situations of greater or lesser emergency, it is possible to decide which laws must remain in force, and which laws may be temporarily relaxed. It should be remembered too that the distinction between scriptural and rabbinical laws is not a rigid one, since, in many instances, it is a matter of *halakhic* debate whether a given law should be placed in one of these categories or the other. Thus, it is far from being beyond the bounds of possibility that a conference of rabbis might remove a law from the status of *deoraita* to that of *derabanan*.

Given all these sources of flexibility and opportunities for change in traditional *halakhah*, it may well be correct for Progressive *halakhah* to regard itself as traditional, rather than as innovative. Indeed, it is innovative to treat all categories of *halakhah* as equal, or as insusceptible of change through discussion, except in the direction of greater severity and rigidity.

Nevertheless, the tension between flexibility and rigidity can be observed also in the past history of the *halakhah*; so that a more accurate assessment might be that certain kinds of modern Neo-Orthodoxy are allying themselves to the severest strand of past *halakhic* opinion, while Progressive *halakhah* (including the Progressive Orthodoxy of such figures as Eliezer Berkovits, Irving Greenberg and David Hartman) allies itself to the more lenient strands. Sometimes this may mean reviving a minority opinion; more often, as in the aspect of *halakhah* to be examined here, it means reviving a majority lenient opinion that has been suppressed in ultra-Orthodoxy. But in all cases, it is right that the past history of the *halakhah* should be searched, not merely to provide justification for modern attitudes, but as a means of defending the Jewish record. For it would be quite wrong to abandon the Jewish past as a source of inspiration, and to regard ourselves as creating a new type of Jewish religion. As a historian of Judaism, I feel that such despair of the Jewish past is unjustified, and that, on the contrary, we should take pride in the traditional *halakhah*, which demands defence against the misrepresentations of obscurantists.

The history of the *halakhah* in relation to sex ethics is a good example of the process by which a basic liberalism has had to be defended against a tendency to introduce undue severity. A paradigm case of the confrontation between sexual liberalism and illiberalism is found in the Talmud itself, in the disagreement between Rabbi Johanan ben Dahabai and the Sages (Nedarim 20b). Here Rabbi Johanan ben Dahabai shows a puritan desire to restrict modes of sexual enjoyment, while the Sages assert that there are no such restrictions. Despite the fact that Rabbi Johanan claims the authority of the Ministering Angels and also makes terrifying assertions about the physical consequences to progeny of out-of-the-ordinary sexual practices, the Sages, i.e. the decisive majority, reject his proposed *halakhah* utterly. Yet later medieval rabbis, while reluctantly accepting the Sages' ruling, show a tendency to return to the attitude of Rabbi Johanan, if only by way of a counsel of perfection - and such supererogatory recommendations can soon assume the status of the norm, especially under the unconscious influence of Christian puritanism, which introduced regulations into canon law that recall Rabbi Johanan's demands.

In general, the Jewish attitude to sex, as expressed in the Hebrew Bible and in Talmudic *halakhah*, is in many respects more positive and liberal than that found in classical Christianity. Sex, in Judaism, is regarded as a healthy and normal human activity. At the same time, it is always acknowledged that the peculiar strength of the sexual drive is a source of special moral dangers. The history of the *halakhah* on sex reflects, indeed, the constant attempt to achieve balance between these two perceptions, both of which are essentially valid.

Attitudes towards pre-marital sexual relations (*biyat penuyah*) form a good example of this pattern of tension between a basic liberalism and a caution that can develop into extreme puritanism. In both Bible and Talmud, pre-marital sex, whether for a man or for a woman, is not regarded as a serious offence; yet in some strains of medieval *halakhic* thought (based on questionable interpretations of certain Talmudic passages), pre-marital sex has become so serious that it is included in the offenses for the avoidance of which martyrdom is required, and is therefore regarded as on a par with murder and idolatry. Yet central *halakhic* authorities remained unaffected by this extremist development, and continued to insist, on the basis of ample Biblical and Talmudic precedent, that pre-marital sex is not a serious offence.

1. *Bible* In the Bible, the most serious offenses are punishable by death or *karet*, and the less serious ones by flogging (*malkut*). Among sexual offenses, adultery, incest and sodomy

133

come into the former category, and prostitution into the latter. A pre-marital sexual act that is not a part of a pattern of prostitution is nowhere assigned any criminal form of punishment, though it may be regarded as an act causing civil damage to the woman involved, and to her family,and therefore incurring reparation from the man. Three kinds of pre-marital sex (other than prostitution) are envisaged: seduction, rape and concubinage. In both seduction and rape, the woman is regarded as the victim of the man, who must offer reparation, either in monetary form, or by marrying the woman, if she so desires. In concubinage (*pilegesh*), where a stable extra-marital relationship is set up between a man (married or unmarried) and a fully consenting unmarried woman, there is no penalty.

Certain Biblical passages are often cited (especially in feminist literature) in attempts to show that the Bible does regard pre-marital sex as a criminal offence for women. The cases of the priest's daughter (Leviticus 21:9) and of the "damsel" (Deuteronomy 22:20) are often taken to assign the death-penalty to women who have engaged in pre-marital sex, but if this were the correct interpretation, how could we understand the law of the "seducer" (Exodus 22:15)? How could a seducer be compelled to marry or compensate a seduced woman if she were regarded as subject to penalty of death? Far from being so regarded, she is treated as a victim, and her loss of virginity is ascribed, through the use of the word *yefateh*, to the initiative of the man, who persuaded her to yield by promises of marriage. Consequently, the rabbis interpret the cases of the priest's daughter   and the "damsel" as concerned with a married woman, who, after the preliminary stage of marriage (*erusin*) remained by custom in her father's house for a year before entering her new home. If she engaged in extra-marital sex during this year, she was guilty of adultery, a capital offence.

Similar remarks apply to the case of the putatively raped woman (Deut. 22:23-24), except that here it is explicitly said that she is both a "virgin" and "betrothed". A presumption of rape is sufficient to clear her (this is given further elaboration in rabbinic law). The common misapprehension that this passage refers to an unmarried woman again arises from ignorance of the ancient form of marriage, in which a married woman remained in her father's home for the period of *erusin*, which counted fully as marriage. If rape is diagnosed, the woman is innocent, and the man guilty of adultery. If, however, the woman is unmarried, no possible charge can be brought against her, while the man, as rabbinic law spells out, in addition to his special Biblical obligation of reparation, has to pay damages as in any other case of physical assault (Ketubot 3:4). Thus an unmarried woman, whether willing or raped, incurs no penalty, while a man who seduces or rapes an unmarried woman is subject to penalties for the damage he has caused to the woman, but has not criminally violated the sexual code itself, which contains no prohibition against pre-marital sex except in the form of prostitution (Deut. 23:17). In other words, pre-marital sex does not constitute a forbidden union, and is frowned on only as a special case of damages for which compensation must be paid to the injured party. This is why concubinage is permissible, for here an unmarried woman has agreed to enter into an extra-marital sexual relationship, and not to regard herself as an injured party.

2. *Talmudic law* The above summary of Biblical law could not avoid some reference to the Talmud, since the Biblical text is so succinct that it cannot be understood without interpretation. Now, however, we turn to Talmudic law in the sense of legislation, rather than exegesis. The rabbis made logical deductions from the Biblical text, and these deductions reinforce the basic liberalism of the Bible's attitude toward pre-marital sex.

Thus the Talmud rules that the offspring of an unmarried woman (*penuyah*) is not a *mamzer*. This means that illegitimacy, in Judaism, has a very different connotation from that found in non-Jewish law. The child of an unmarried woman is not illegitimate and has no legal disabilities whatever. His/her rights of inheritance from his/her father are the same as those of a child born in wedlock. His/her rights of marriage have no limitations; he/she can marry, for example, into the priesthood. Since illegitimacy or *mamzerut* is an outcome of the illegitimacy of the sexual relation giving rise to it (i.e. incest or adultery), the legitimacy of the child of an unmarried woman testifies completely to the legitimacy of pre-marital relations.

Even more striking is the Talmudic ruling (Yebamot 61b) that a woman who has engaged in a pre-marital sexual relation has not thereby disqualified herself from subsequent marriage to a priest. Here the question at issue is less clearcut than the question of whether the child of such a union is a *mamzer*, which is very easily answered in the negative without any dissentient opinion. For the status of *zonah*, by which a woman becomes disqualified for marriage to a priest through some kind of irregular sexual experience, is subject to disagreement. One authority, Rabbi Eliezer, indeed, does hold that a woman who has had unmarried sexual relations is disqualified in this context. But the authoritative majority opinion is that such a woman is not a *zonah*. Thus, though unmarried sex is certainly regarded as in some degree irregular, it is not sufficiently so to change the marital status of a woman.

To what extent, then, does the talmud disapprove of pre-marital sex? This question really amounts to asking, "What is the status of concubinage in Talmudic law?" For pre-marital sex brought about by deception or force employed against the woman is covered by the Biblical laws which provide for compensation to

136

the woman, regarded as wronged by the man. The question, however, is whether pre-marital sex (other than prostitution) in which the woman gives her full consent, is forbidden, and if so, in what degree of seriousness. The exact answer to this question is not very easy to find in the talmud. Certain passages certainly seem to indicate a strong disapproval of such relations; yet when we seek to quantify this disapproval in terms of the main categories of legal importance, we meet with difficulties. Thus we find some surprising differences of opinion on this topic among the interpreters of the Talmud, the *rishonim* and the *aharonim*, down to the present day. Two cryptic Talmudic passages, now to be discussed, are at the root of the severest strain of opinion; but the general evidence of leniency found in both Bible and Talmud, as outlined above, have kept mainstream commentators from interpreting even these passages in an extreme sense.

The main Talmudic passage that seems to stand contrary to all the indications of leniency in other passages is the story found in the Babylonian Talmud Sanhedrin 75a. This story tells of a man who "conceived a passion for a certain woman, and his heart was consumed by his burning desire. When the doctors were consulted, they said, 'His only cure is that she shall submit.' Thereupon the Sages said: 'Let him die rather than that she should yield.' Then said the doctors, 'Let her stand nude before him '; they answered, 'Sooner let him die.' 'Then', said the doctors, 'let her converse with him from behind a fence.' 'Let him die,' the Sages replied, 'rather than she should converse with him from behind the fence.'" The woman, according to one Talmudic authority, though not according to others, was unmarried.

This story appears to mean that any sexual impropriety, however trivial (e.g. conversing with an unmarried woman from behind a fence without matrimonial intent) is to be regarded as so serious that one must undergo death rather than perform it. If this is the correct interpretation of the story, then the whole scale of *halakhic* values found elsewhere in the Talmud is overturned. According to the well-known decision of the rabbis (Sanhedrin 74a), only three offenses were serious enough to require martyrdom: murder, *gilui arayot*, and idolatry. These three offenses, if committed voluntarily, incur the severest penalty, that of death, but even in this category, they are more serious than other capital offenses, for which martyrdom is not required. Yet in the story quoted above, this decision seems to be ignored, and offenses which cannot be regarded by any stretch of the imagination as capital, or even as incurring *malkut*, are declared to require *mesirat nefesh*.

This story, consequently, was found very puzzling, and in order to explain it, an adjunct Talmudic passage was adduced: "It was asked of R. Ammi: Is a Noachide bound to sanctify the Divine Name or not? Abaye said, Come and hear: The Noachides were commanded to keep seven precepts. Now, if they were commanded to sanctify the Divine Name, there are eight. Rava said to him: Them, and all pertaining thereto (*inhu vekhol abizraihu*)."

The interpretation offered of this remark of Rava's was that those obliged to incur martyrdom rather than commit one of the three cardinal offenses should do so not only if the offence presents itself in its most culpable form, but even in its less serious forms. Thus, for example, to commit adultery is a capital offence, and rather than commit this offence, martyrdom is obviously required. But the doctrine of *abizraihu*, on this interpretation, also requires martyrdom for lesser offenses that are in some way connected with adultery: for example, the offence of embracing and fondling another man's wife, which is regarded as Biblically forbidden (on pain of *malkut*) by Lev. 18: 6. Confirmation of this interpretation was found in relation to the laws of idolatry: for there was evidence that *mesirat nefesh* was required not merely for capital offenses in this category, but also for less serious offenses (Pesahim 25a, and comments of Ran). As far as I am aware, however, no attempt was made to add lesser categories to the requirement of martyrdom for murder, though in theory such categories would not be hard to find (e.g. giving information leading to someone's death).

It is doubtful whether this interpretation would ever have been given to the passage about *abizraihu* had it not been for the need to give some explanation for the passage about "the man in love", which follows immediately, thus making it plausible that the story was intended as an illustration of the practical application of the concept. For the term *abizraihu* in itself, in the context of the discussion of which it forms a part, does not really lend itself to such an interpretation. The argument in which it is found concerns whether Gentiles obedient to the Noachide laws are required to undergo martyrdom, presumably in relation to the three Noachide laws that coincide with the three martyrdom-requiring laws listed in the decision of Bet Nitza. Abaye objects that his would make the Noachide laws into eight instead of seven, to which Rava very logically replies that this is not so, since the requirement of martyrdom is not an extra commandment but is an *implication* of the others. In other words, since the Noachides laws have been given all three of the commandments that require martyrdom, they have also been given the requirement to undergo martyrdom for them, since this requirement is inseparable from them. Thus Rava's use of the term *abizraihu* ("their appurtenances") does not intend to introduce any other commandments, but only the logical implications of these three commandments themselves. To go beyond this and say that Rava meant to introduce a swarm of other lesser commandments as requiring martyrdom is to interpret his words in a very strained manner.

It is noteworthy that this unconvincing interpretation of *abizraihu* is not found in the Geonic writings, or in Maimonides or in Rashi or Tosafot; it is found first in the writings of 13th century Rishonim. Rashi indeed interprets *abizraihu* in the sense suggested above, as referring only to logical implication. Yet once introduced, the doctrine of *abizraihu* receives further elaboration. The question is asked whether there is any limit at all to the sexual commandments included as requiring martyrdom. Does this requirement extend only to Biblical negative commandments such as *lo tikrevu* (Lev. 18: 6, see above), or does it extend even to rabbinical regulations, such as the prohibition against being alone (*yihud*) with an unmarried woman? Some authorities are willing to extend the doctrine of *abizraihu* even as far as this, chiefly because otherwise it seems hard to explain the story of "the man in love", where no biblical prohibition seems to be involved. Others resist this extreme conclusion, finding it incredible that martyrdom should be required for such trivial reasons, especially as even intercourse with an unmarried woman (never mind *yihud*) cannot be regarded as biblically prohibited, and only with difficulty as even rabbinically prohibited. The influence of the story of "the man in love" can even be discerned in the increasing tendency to argue that intercourse with an unmarried woman is indeed biblically forbidden, falling within the definition of "prostitution"; this involves the denial that concubinage is permitted either by biblical or rabbinical law, a conclusion very hard to reconcile with obvious sources.

All this increasing severity can be traced to the need to understand this one Talmudic passage, the story of "the man in love", because the other passage, on *abizraihu*, only entered the argument as allegedly providing the rationale of that story. When one considers that the *abizraihu* passage is actually concerned with non-Jews, it becomes even more incredible that it should be meant to extend the obligation to martyrdom even to rabbinical laws; for surely non-Jews are never under any obligation to observe rabbinical enactments. But even if one takes the view that only Biblical prohibitions such as *lo tikrevu* are being added to the requirement for martyrdom, the idea is most implausible in relation to non-Jews, who are not required to observe those sexual prohibitions (*lavin*) that carry no death penalty. Thus even the prohibition against prostitution does not apply to non-Jews, not being included in the Noachide laws, and indeed expressly excluded from the requirement of non-Jewish observance by the Bible itself when it says, "There shall be no prostitute among the daughters of Israel" (Deut. 23: 17). Yet if *abizraihu* carries the suggested meaning, even non-Jews are obliged to undergo martyrdom for the most trivial sexual improprieties. Indeed any unprejudiced reading of the *abizraihu* passage will lead to the conclusion that it is intended to reduce the number of commandments laid upon non-Jews rather than increase them. Abaye is objecting that Noachides are subject to only seven commandments, not more, while Rava agrees with this, but points out that there are implications of these seven that do not constitute separate commandments. Yet, under the influence of another Talmudic passage, the medieval commentators produce a proliferation of Noachide commandments which makes the Noachides subject not only to biblical *lavin*, but even, on some interpretations, to minute rabbinical regulations! Any convincing interpretation of the *abizraihu* passage must surely allow it to apply with some plausibility to non-Jews, with whom it is chiefly concerned.

Thus we are left with the passage about "the man in love" as our main problem, and we may now ask the question, "What does this story really mean?" An unprejudiced re-reading of the story leads to the conclusion that this story is really irrelevant to the question, "Which sexual offenses are serious enough to require martyrdom?" What the story is really telling us is that no woman is required to sacrifice her status or dignity for the sake of a madman. If the cure prescribed by the doctors had involved some infringement of *halakhah* not involving any other person (e.g. the eating of forbidden substances by the afflicted man), then the Rabbis no doubt would have permitted this. But an alleged cure (the end of the *sugya* suggests that it would not even have worked!) that requires some other person to make a serious sacrifice of status or dignity does not come into the category of cures that demand a relaxation of *halakhah* however small. Thus no conclusions relating to the law of martyrdom in general (or the related law of *pikuah nefesh*) can be drawn from this case, which must be regarded as a special case - indeed it can be regarded as an illustration of a kind of case in which the concept of *pikuah nefesh* does not apply. We might generalize this case as follows: "If some person tells me that unless I do something (that I do not want to do or that I disapprove of doing) he will die, and there is no reasonable ground for this request, I have no obligation to accede to this request, even if, in fact, his death will result. If the thing requested is actually undesirable from a social point of view, I have an obligation *not* to do it, even if his death will result." In other words, people should not be blackmailed into unwelcome or undesirable acts of *any* kind by a threat of suicide whether deliberate or involuntary. Thus the decision of the rabbis in the case of "the man in love" was not dictated by ultra-puritanism, but by the application of the above principle against blackmail.

This analysis is substantially the same as that offered by the Bet Shemuel on *Even Haezer* 20:1. His view of the "man in love" story is that it comes into the category of *migdar milta* (an extraordinary measure from which no analogies can be drawn, see Yebamot, 90b.). The Rabbis decreed that where undesirable social consequences may follow, a person cannot be required to sacrifice dignity or status even where this may lead to the saving of another person's life. The matter is not one of transgression (*averah*) but of loss of status (*pegam*). The Beit Shemuel concludes, therefore, that in the different case where a person is given a choice by a tyrant, "transgress or die," even intercourse (never mind *yihud*) with an unmarried woman is not a matter for *mesirat nefesh*. "In the case of an unmarried woman, we do not say, 'He should die rather than transgress'." This is because Beit Shemuel regards intercourse with an unmarried woman as not Biblically forbidden, and he regards the doctrine of *abizraihu* (which he accepts) as applying only to Biblically-forbidden transgressions. Thus Beit Shemuel rejects the view that the story of "the man in love" implies that all sexual offenses (even *yihud* with an unmarried woman) require *mesirat nefesh*. Similar to the standpoint of the Beit Shemuel is that of the Shakh; while in opposition to these relatively moderate views stands the Vilna Gaon, who indeed holds that it is required to give one's life rather than to transgress even a rabbinical laws in sexual matters.

The question, however, arises, "Why does the man-in-love story appear where it does, following the *abizraihu* passage, unless the two passages are closely connected in thought?" On the analysis given above, there seems little connection between the two passages, since the first, the *abizraihu* passage, deals only with the martyrdom requirement for Gentiles for major transgressions (not with a martyrdom requirement for both Jews and Gentiles for minor transgressions), while the second (the man-in-love story) deals with a case where considerations of *pikuah nefesh* do not apply. On the above argument, a spurious connection has been made traditionally between the two passages by taking the first passage to refer to minor transgressions, and by taking the second passage to refer to a necessity of martyrdom for very minor transgressions indeed.

The answer is that, given the loose association between succeeding passages in the Talmud generally, no very specific connection is required. One passage deals with martyrdom; this suggests the related topic of *pikuah nefesh* (related because a mortally sick man who refuses or is refused medical aid that involves a forbidden act of one of the three main types is a kind of martyr), and this suggests an unusual type of case where a sick man begs for a remedy of a doubtful kind and this had to be refused, though the infringement was not of a serious kind. Such tenuous links are common enough in Talmudic sequences. The very specific link found between the two passages from the 13th century on is based on wrong interpretations of both.

It appears, then, from the above discussion, that the task of Progressive *halakhah* may sometimes be to rescue the Talmud from some of its medieval commentators. The Talmud itself has a lenient view about pre-marital sex, which it rates as at most rabbinically forbidden. But medieval commentators, by misapprehending the passages about *abizraihu* and the man-in-love story, and running them together as if they formed one topic, foisted an uncharacteristic puritanism on the Talmud, and wound up (in the case of some commentators) with regarding pre-marital sex and even lesser misdemeanors as on a par with adultery, incest, idolatry and murder; so that no allowances could be made, in the case of emergency, for gradation of importance in sexual offenses. The result of this *halakhic* process can be seen in modern times, when Orthodox authorities, basing themselves on the severest medieval interpretations of *abizraihu*, have refused to make distinctions between pre-marital sex and fundamental sexual sins when faced with the emergency of AIDS. It is necessary to return to the flexibility of both Bible and Talmud, and the essential basis of such flexibility is the preservation of distinctions between the graver and the lighter transgressions, as well as an awareness of the past history of variety of opinion among exponents of the *halakhah*.

NOTE ON MAIMONIDES

Maimonides changed his mind on the issue of pre-marital relations. In the first version of his Commentary on the Mishnah, he wrote, "Intercourse with an unmarried woman incurs a punishment of rabbinical flogging; and the proof that this is a rabbinical prohibition is that she is not disqualified from marrying a priest, and is not called *zonah*. If this were biblically forbidden, she would be forbidden to a priest as in the case of all negative commandments" (*M*. Sanhedrin, 7:3). Later he crossed this out and substituted, "Intercourse with an unmarried woman incurs flogging (*malkut*) even though she is not disqualified from marrying a priest and is not called a *zonah*." He gives no reason for this change of mind. In the *Mishneh Torah* (Ishut 1:4), he apparently says that all unmarried intercourse is biblically forbidden and the woman involved is a *kedeshah* by virtue of this one act of intercourse. See the criticism of Ravad *ad loc*. See Joseph Kafah's commentary on the *Mishneh Torah ad loc*. (Jerusalem 1987).

Many commentators have pointed out the difficulties in Maimonides' final position arising from the biblical law of seduction. As for the difficulties arising from the permitted biblical status of *pilegesh*, some commentators argue that *pilegesh* does not mean "unmarried concubine" but "married without a ketubah" (relying here on a conjectural reading of Sanh. 21a as apparently read by Rashi on Gen. 25:6). Yet Maimonides himself does not define *pilegesh* in this way (*Mishneh Torah* Hil. Melakhim 4:4). Nahmanides held that *pilegesh* means "unmarried concubine" and is permitted both by biblical and rabbinical law - though he advised that this should not be publicized, because of the danger of infringement of *nidah* (see *Otzar Haposkim* on Even Haezer 26:1).

It is noteworthy that Maimonides does not adduce in support of his final position either the doctrine of *abizraihu* (not mentioned anywhere in his writings) or the case of "the man in love". He does mention the latter case (*Misneh Torah* Hil. Yesodei Hatorah 5: 9), but only as a special enactment of the Rabbis, not as the basis of general conclusions about pre-marital sexual relations.

There have been great disagreements among *poskim* both about what Maimonides really meant and about the issue of *pilegesh* itself. In the words of *Otzar Haposkim*, "Isserles distinguishes two opinions in relation to *pilegesh*: 1. that it is permitted; 2. that it incurs *malqut* because of the prohibition of prostitution. But there are also many other views among the *posqim*: 1. that it is not forbidden because of prostitution but because of transgression of the positive commandment of formal marriage; 2. that it is forbidden not biblically but rabbinically; 3. that it is not actually forbidden, but is disapproved of. And there are also many other differences of opinion." Jacob Emden even regarded the *pilegesh*-relationship as praiseworthy in certain circumstances. It has also been doubted whether Maimonides really meant to characterize all instances of pre-marital intercourse as prostitution (see *Radbaz*, 4:225, who makes a distinction between casual sex and a stable unmarried relationship, and argues that Maimonides was referring only to the former). For a full discussion of the range of opinions see *Otzar Haposkim*, Even Haezer 26:1.

Contributors

Haim H. Cohn - Retired 1981 from the Supreme Court of Israel after more than twenty years as Associate Justice and Deputy President. Earlier, he served as Israel's Attorney General and Minister of Justice. In addition to his mastery of secular law, he pursued rabbinical studies at Yeshivat Merkaz Ha Rav (Jerusalem). Among his many works are *Jewish Law in Ancient and Modern Israel* (1971), *The Trial and Death of Jesus* (1968, 1971), and *Human Rights in Jewish Law* (1984).

Walter Jacob - Rabbi, Rodef Shalom Congregation, Pittsburgh, President Elect, Central Conference of American Rabbis, Chairman of the Freehof Institute of Progressive Halakhah. Author and editor of fourteen books including *American Reform Responsa* (1983), and *Contemporary American Reform Responsa* (1987), *Liberal Judaism and Halakhah* (1988), *New Reform Responsa* (1991).

Hyam Maccoby - Teacher at the Leo Baeck College, London. He is the author of many books, including *Judaism on Trial* (1982), *The Mythmaker* (1986), *Early Rabbinic Writings* (1988), *Paul and Hellenism* (1991).

John D. Rayner - A graduate of Cambridge University and Hebrew Union College, Rabbi Emeritus of the Liberal Jewish Synagogue, London, England, and Lecturer in Liturgy and Codes at Leo Baeck College.

W. Gunther Plaut - Senior Scholar at Holy Blossom Temple, Toronto, Canada, author of seventeen books, the editor and principal author of *The Torah - A Modern Commentary*, a past president of the Central Conference of American Rabbis. He is the current chairperson of its Responsa Committee.

Mark Washofsky - Associate Professor of Rabbinics - Hebrew Union College-Jewish Institute of Religion in Cincinnati. His publications include studies on the development of *halakhic* thought in medieval and modern times. He currently serves as vice chair of the Responsa Committee of the Central Conference of American Rabbis.

Moshe Zemer - Director of the Freehof Institute of Progressive *Halakhah*; a founder of the Movement for Progressive Judaism in Israel; *Av Bet Din* of the Israel Council of Progressive Rabbis; founding rabbi of Kedem Synagogue in Tel Aviv; author of forthcoming the book, *The Sane Halakhah* (Hebrew).

148